# Three Plays

by

Zetta Elliott

Copyright © 2008 Zetta Elliott

## Table of Contents

Connor's Boy…………………………………………...1

Mother Load…..…………………………………55

Beast………………………………………...…115

A Talk with the Playwright……………………185

**CONNOR'S BOY**

A Play

by

Zetta Elliott

Copyright © 2008 Zetta Elliott

*Connor's Boy* was selected for Karamu Theatre's R. Joyce Whitley Festival of New Plays ARENAFEST, and was staged in Cleveland, OH on January 10 & 17, 2008.

*Connor's Boy* was also selected for the Maieutic Theatre's Newborn Festival, and was staged in New York City on January 24, 2008.

# CONNOR'S BOY

## Synopsis:

A writer, Simone, falls in love with an artist, Connor, while collaborating on a picture book for children. He is a single parent of a three-year old son, Malik; Simone never wanted to have children, but is irresistibly drawn to the pair. As their intimacy grows, Connor confesses to Simone that he was abused as a child. Adopted by a white family as an infant, Connor was "returned" to the adoption agency at age five when his adoptive parents divorced. He then spent the next thirteen years moving from one foster home to another. Although he reconnected with his white adoptive brother later in life, Connor resents the family who rejected him because of his race. As Connor goes through the process of recovery, Simone grows uncomfortable with Connor's close relationship with his son. Doubting her own ability to be a good mother, she breaks off her engagement with Connor and foolishly shares her fears with her agent, who contacts Children's Services; when his son is taken into protective custody, Connor loses his battle with depression and commits suicide.

The play begins on the day of Connor's funeral. His former adoptive mother, Elinore, arrives with her two grown biological children, Michael and Deborah. Michael resents his mother for reversing her adoption of Connor; when her marriage failed, Elinore chose to take her own children from Connecticut to California to build a new life. Deborah is determined to take custody of Malik, but she is challenged by Simone, who is now reconsidering her position on parenting and has the backing of Connor's birth mother, Marva. Connor's sudden death forces the people who loved him to confront each other, the past, and the guilt that fuels their fierce struggle over his child.

## List of Characters:

**Simone:** a black woman writer; former fiancée of Connor Fitzgerald; prior to Connor's suicide, Simone called off their engagement as she grew uncomfortable with Connor's extremely close relationship with his son.

> Now that Connor is gone, Simone does not want any of Connor's white adoptive relatives to gain custody of Malik, but feels guilty and fears she is inadequate to raise him herself.

**Elinore:** former adoptive white mother of Connor; a sophisticated, older woman; proud liberal; suppressed hysteric

**Michael:** adoptive brother of Connor; resents his mother for separating the children during the divorce; opposes his sister's bid to adopt the child; an alcoholic, like his father

**Deborah:** adoptive sister of Connor; she and her lesbian lover want to adopt Malik as a way of making amends for Elinore's rejection of Connor

**Malik:** Connor's three-year old son

**Ruth:** agent of Connor and Simone; a white, middle-aged woman; savvy but tactless at times.

**Marva:** Connor's birth mother; a working class black woman, former drug addict, and born-again Christian

**Barlow:** Connor's birth father; a humble yet dignified older black man; like Marva, a former addict, now a deacon in his church

**Irene:** Simone's snobbish mother; a sophisticated, upper middle-class black woman

## SETTING

An apartment in Brooklyn.

## TIME

Now.

## ACT I

## Scene 1

[*Music: John Coltrane's "A Love Supreme." We see, dimly lit, Simone in her bed; she is restless, her sleep disturbed by memories and the "ghosts" moving through the woods behind her. The backdrop should be dark, the silhouette of trees visible, with occasional silvery white birches. Between these roam the shadows from Connor's studio—muted, sheer streams of color. Connor should roam with them—a lingering presence, not necessarily human/male. LIGHTS UP as a bell rings loudly. Simone, in bed, starts as if woken cruelly from a dream. She reaches for her alarm clock and realizes the phone is also ringing. She silences the alarm, the bell stops ringing, and she answers the phone.*]

SIMONE: [*Surly, groggy.*] What?

RUTH: Simone? Is that you?

SIMONE: [*She takes the phone with her as she withdraws under the covers.*] What do you want?

RUTH: Simone, it's me, Ruth. You asked me to call, remember? You didn't want to sleep too late…you said the medication made you drowsy.

SIMONE: [*Reaches for a bottle of prescribed sedatives by her bed. In a more conciliatory tone.*] Oh…right. Sorry, Ruth. I must have been dreaming…

RUTH: It's ok. [*Pause.*] You remember what day it is, right?

SIMONE: Tuesday…?

RUTH: Simone, today's the funeral--Connor's funeral. Can you get dressed and be ready in an hour? I'll swing by around ten. [*Pause.*] Simone?

SIMONE: Connor's…gone. I must have been dreaming.

RUTH: Are you up, Simone?

SIMONE: [*She burrows deeper into the bed.*] Yes.

RUTH: And you'll be ready in an hour?

SIMONE: Yes.

RUTH: Oh, Simone. I can only imagine how hard this must be for you. Connor was a brilliant artist, and…[*She falters.*] …a very *special* person. And you must know that I've always thought of you as so much more than a client. You're—like a daughter to me. [*Pause.*] You know, Simone, you don't have to go…

SIMONE: [*She instantly rouses herself.*] No! I mean, I do. I have to be there.

RUTH: Alright. Then I'll see you at ten?

SIMONE: I'll wait for you downstairs. [*She throws back the covers, hangs up the phone, and sits on the edge of the bed. Simone reaches for a framed photograph on the bedside table. She examines it dully, before setting it face down and rising from the bed. Lights down.*]

## ACT I

## Scene 2

[*Lights up on a crowded room, possibly the basement of a church. Food-laden tables are draped with white table cloths, and people talk in clusters, in hushed tones. Solemn hymns are being played on an organ. The vast majority of people are black; the two white siblings stand out, and appear self-conscious even as they try to act relaxed.*]

DEBORAH: Connor would have hated this.

MICHAEL: How the fuck would you know?

DEBORAH: He was an atheist, wasn't he?

MICHAEL: Muslim—he converted a few months ago.

DEBORAH: Then I don't see why they had to hold the reception in a church.

MICHAEL: [*Takes a flask from inside his jacket and spikes his drink.*] Sinners are always squeamish in the house of God. Is that why you didn't bring Allie? Thought it was best to leave her back home in the closet?

DEBORAH: I see you started earlier than usual today.

MICHAEL: Fuck you, Deb.

DEBORAH: Just like dear old Dad. You're a real chip off the old block, Mike.

MICHAEL: It's a wake. You're supposed to have a few drinks, share a few memories. Christ…lighten up.

DEBORAH: Well, I'm sure you'll be high as a kite in no time. Where's Mom?

MICHAEL: How the hell should I know? I thought you were babysitting her today.

DEBORAH: It's always *my* job, isn't it. You don't give a damn if she makes a fool of herself.

MICHAEL: Neither do you. You're just trying to cover your own ass. Admit it—you're ashamed of her, too.

DEBORAH: She means well, but this whole…*event* has thrown her off balance.

MICHAEL: Event? This isn't a fucking event, Deb. It's a funeral. Our brother's funeral! [*Drains his glass.*]

DEBORAH: For God's sake, Michael, keep your voice down! The last thing these people want is for us to cause a scene.

MICHAEL: These people? *These people?*

DEBORAH: Michael, please!

MICHAEL: Sssshhhh—quiet, Deb. We've got to keep this on the "down low"—that's black for hush-hush. Connor—our brother—our dead brother….was a NEGRO!

DEBORAH: [*Hisses.*] Oh—my—God. I can't believe you're doing this. You say you loved him, you flew halfway across the country just to be here, and this is how you act!

MICHAEL: [*Sobers somewhat.*] I did love him. I always loved him, even after…. He used to call me Mikey…

DEBORAH: Where could she have gone off to? Stay here and keep an eye out. I'm going to look in the ladies room.

MICHAEL: Did you check the kiddie table? She's probably over there trying seduce another innocent little pickaninny.

DEBORAH: You're a disgrace, Michael. An absolute disgrace.

MICHAEL: I'm proud of you, too, Deb. It's an honor to share your lovely lesbian DNA.

DEBORAH: [*Vicious, but low.*] They should have sent you back, not Connor. Why couldn't we get a refund on YOU?

MICHAEL: Because I'm your blood brother, baby. And blood is thicker than…

DEBORAH: [*Spots her mother and tries to discreetly wave her over.*] Mom! Mom!

ELINORE: There you are, I was wondering where you'd gone off to.

DEBORAH: You disappeared.

ELINORE: Don't be silly, Deborah. I was just talking to some old friends. There are faces here I haven't seen in nearly thirty years.

MICHAEL: It's just like your high school reunion, huh, Mom? Only you could put the "fun" in funeral.

DEBORAH: Ignore him, Mom. He's drunk.

ELINORE: Oh, Michael.

MICHAEL: Let's have a toast, shall we? To Connor—the best little brother I ever had. Or almost had…

ELINORE: Michael, please. This isn't the time or the place…

MICHAEL: Connor's DEAD, Mother. We just put him in the ground. Don't tell me when and where it's okay to claim him. We wouldn't be here today if you hadn't denied him all those years ago…

DEBORAH: Michael!

MICHAEL: You killed him, you narcissistic bitch! YOU KILLED MY BABY BROTHER!

SIMONE: [*Approaches them with a stony face.*] Perhaps it would be best if you left now.

ELINORE: Simone! I'm so sorry, dear—Michael's just—he's upset, you know. He's taking it hard, Connor's death…

SIMONE: Still, it might be best if…

DEBORAH: He was part of our family, too, you know. We have a right to be here.

SIMONE: [*Pause. Simone steels herself against an impulse to strike her. She wraps her arms around herself.*] I'm not going to argue with you, Deborah. But I'm also not about to stand here and let you ruin this day for everyone else. I've had enough of your family's dysfunction.

DEBORAH: Where's Malik?

SIMONE: What?

DEBORAH: Connor's son—where is he?

SIMONE: [*Warily.*] He's not here.

DEBORAH: Why?

SIMONE: He couldn't come.

ELINORE: What a shame. I was so looking forward to meeting him.

SIMONE: He doesn't know anything about you. Connor wanted it that way.

DEBORAH: Connor's not here anymore. What's going to happen to his son?

SIMONE: That's not your concern.

DEBORAH: We're his family. We have a right to know where you're keeping Malik.

SIMONE: I'm not keeping him anywhere. But if it were up to me, I'd sure as hell keep him away from you. You're like a virus, the lot of you. You kill every black child you come in contact with.

DEBORAH: You should know I've hired a lawyer.

ELINORE: Deborah!

DEBORAH: She can't keep him from us, Mom. Malik isn't here today because he's in foster care. They took him away from her.

MICHAEL: Is that true?

SIMONE: I think you should go now.

ELINORE: What happened to the child? [*With rising hysteria.*] What did you do to him?

SIMONE: Get them out of here, Michael.

MICHAEL: Alright, let's just go. We can talk about this another time.

DEBORAH: You'll be hearing from my attorney.

[*They exit, Deborah and Elinore indignant; Michael sad and shamed. Simone watches them go, her face filled with rage and fear.*]

MARVA: [*Approaches Simone from behind and wraps an arm around her waist.*] You alright, baby?

SIMONE: [*Remains tense and steps away from Marva's concern.*] I'm fine.

MARVA: You don't look fine. You look like one a them cobras, about to strike. That was them?

SIMONE: That was them.

MARVA: They got a lotta nerve, showing up here and making a scene. My church family don't know what to think—white folks walking up in here, acting crazy when I just put my son in the ground.

SIMONE: Why don't you explain it to them, Marva? Tell them just why those crazy white folks were here.

MARVA: [*Surprised by Simone's hostility.*] Well, I—I…it ain't like I mind them coming here to pay their respects. Connor meant something to them, I understand that. But that whiteboy—he looked like he had too much to drink, and that other one—she looked like she wanted to start something with you. I'd've come over sooner, but I didn't want to cause no more drama…

SIMONE: Of course. I understand.

MARVA: You know you're like a daughter to me, Simone. I know you and Connor would have been so happy together.

SIMONE: Maybe. Maybe not.

MARVA: [*Taken aback again.*] What do you mean? I know my boy died before he got a chance to say "I do," but he meant for you to be his wife. He even showed me the ring.

SIMONE: I gave it back.

MARVA: What? Why?

SIMONE: Because I couldn't marry him, Marva.

MARVA: Why not? All of a sudden you too good for my boy?

SIMONE: [*Shakes her head sadly.*] I was never good enough…

REVEREND: Excuse me, Sister Marva. We're ready whenever you are. If you'd care to say a few words just to start things off…

MARVA: Of course, Reverend Johnson. I'll be right there. [*She turns back to Simone, but Simone has drifted away. Marva perks up, and slips back into the role of the grieving mother. The crowd moves to surround her as she steps up, takes the microphone, and begins to reminisce.*] Brothers and sisters, I'd like to thank you for coming here today to honor the memory of my son, Connor… [*For a moment, her eyes meet Simone's—Marva falters, then Simone exits and Marva regains her confidence and continues her performance.*] Connor left us too soon…

## ACT I

### Scene 3

[*A hotel room, not luxurious but a cut above. There are two double beds separated by a nightstand with a lamp. A table and four chairs stand off to one side, there is a mini bar along the wall. A door in the back leads to the bathroom; a second door leads to the hallway. The*

*Fitzgeralds, still dressed in formal black attire, are discussing the funeral.*]

ELINORE: What a dreadful day!

MICHAEL: [*Takes off his suit jacket, loosens his tie, and opens the small fridge. He begins to pour himself a drink.*] So much for seeing old friends, huh, Mom?

ELINORE: Michael, please, I know you're upset but this drinking has got to stop.

DEBORAH: [*Removes her heels and stockings.*] It's too late, Mom. Mike could drink Dad under the table.

ELINORE: Don't say that, Deborah. [*To* MICHAEL.] You don't have to be like your father, Michael. We can get you some help…

MICHAEL: I don't need help. You mourn your way, [*He toasts them.*] I'll mourn mine. [*He sits alone at the table, staring sullenly into his glass.*]

DEBORAH: I'm going to take a quick shower.

MICHAEL: Feeling dirty? Don't worry, Deb—it doesn't rub off.

DEBORAH: The really sad thing about you, Mike, is that you're an asshole even when you're sober. [*She opens a suitcase and sifts through it, looking for casual clothes.*]

ELINORE: What's happened to my children…you never used to be this way.

DEBORAH: [*Holding her clothes, she heads towards the bathroom door, stopping by the table to hiss at* MICHAEL *first.*] Just leave her alone, Mike! I'm warning you… [*To her mother.*] You must be famished, Mom. Why don't you change and order something from room service.

ELINORE: Yes, I do feel a bit faint. Perhaps some soup…
[DEBORAH *returns to the nightstand, pulls the menu from the drawer and hands it to her mother, who is seated on the foot of the bed.*] Thank you, Deborah. [DEBORAH *glares at* MICHAEL *as she passes him and exits to the bathroom. Soon we hear the sound of the shower running.* MICHAEL *continues to nurse his drink silently. After a*

*moment, he uses the back of his hand to wipe his eyes.*] It was hard for you, wasn't it.

MICHAEL: [*Flatly.*] What?

ELINORE: The divorce, the move. Losing Connor.

MICHAEL: We didn't "lose" Connor, Mom. You sent him back.

ELINORE: I couldn't raise him on my own, Michael.

MICHAEL: Why not? He wasn't disabled—he didn't have "special needs." He was black for Christ's sake! But he was still your son.

ELINORE: Perhaps if your father hadn't…it was his idea, really. I was willing to adopt, but I'd never thought about adopting a colored child…

MICHAEL: So Dad made you do it.

ELINORE: No, that's not what I'm saying. Adopting Connor was—for your father—a political gesture. It was, I think…symbolic, more than anything else.

MICHAEL: That's not true—Dad loved Connor the same way he loved me and Deb.

ELINORE: Perhaps. But in the end, he loved alcohol more. [*Pause.*] I couldn't manage on my own with three children.

MICHAEL: You could have tried. You should have tried. We were the only family he'd ever known…

ELINORE: I thought he'd be better off with…his own kind. I was sure another family would adopt him.

MICHAEL: Well, you were wrong, weren't you.

[*The shower stops, and momentarily* DEBORAH *reenters the room, wearing a white terry robe. She rubs a towel against her wet hair.*]

DEBORAH: Did you order already, Mom?

ELINORE: No, dear, not yet.

DEBORAH: [*Shoots* MICHAEL *a deadly glance.*] You ok?

ELINORE: [*Tries to perk up.*] Yes, of course, I'm just tired.

DEBORAH: Have you taken your medication today?

ELINORE: [*Flushes, embarrassed.*] Yes, Deborah. I took it this morning. [*Clears her throat.*]Shall I order you something?

DEBORAH: Just a salad. I'll be out in a minute. [*She retreats into the bathroom; we hear the sound of a blow dryer.*]

ELINORE: What about you, Michael? Are you hungry? [*She rises from the bed and moves over to the nightstand, where the phone is.*]

MICHAEL: [*He watches her, saddened by her seeming frailty. Then he turns back to his drink.*] I'm good.

ELINORE: [*She dials.*] Yes, room service? [*She orders, then hangs up the phone. She remains seated by the nightstand.*] Did you know your sister was seeking custody of Malik?

MICHAEL: [*Snorts derisively and refills his glass.*] She hasn't got a chance in hell. And I will personally do all I can to ensure Deb never gets her hands on Connor's boy.

ELINORE: I've waited a long time to become a grandmother. [*Laughs lightly.*] I never imagined it would happen this way.

MICHAEL: Ironic, isn't it? You pushed Connor out of the picture, and now his ghost's come back to haunt you.

ELINORE: [*Quietly.*] I wouldn't mind, you know—a black grandchild.

MICHAEL: One generation removed makes it ok? So long as no one thinks it came out of *your* womb.

ELINORE: Times have changed…it's more—common, now. I wouldn't feel—

MICHAEL: Embarrassed? Ashamed?

ELINORE: [*She hardens suddenly.*] I'm human, Michael. I made mistakes. You think I don't have regrets?

MICHAEL: [*He turns back to his drink.*] It's too late for your regrets.

[*The blow dryer stops, and* DEBORAH *reenters the room, this time dressed in jeans and a sweatshirt. It bears the logo of an elite women's college.*]

DEBORAH: Did you order, Mom?

ELINORE: Yes. The food should be here shortly.

DEBORAH: Good, I'm starving! [DEB *plunks down on the bed.*] So. What should we do with the rest of this day? A museum, maybe?

MICHAEL: That's right—let's go sight seeing—or better yet, shopping! What's a trip to New York without a stop at Bloomingdales.

DEBORAH: What would you suggest, Michael? That we sit here and drink ourselves into a stupor with you?

MICHAEL: Do whatever the fuck you want, Deb. In fact, you might as well go shopping for some other little kid, because there's no fucking way you're getting custody of Malik.

DEBORAH: [*Turns first to her mother, looking for support, but* ELINORE *looks away.*] I thought you of all people would want this.

MICHAEL: Why would I want YOU to raise Connor's son?

DEBORAH: It's like a second chance, isn't it? A chance to make things right.

ELINORE: That's a lovely idea, darling, but...don't you think Malik would be better off with his mother?

DEBORAH: He hasn't got a mother. She died less than a year after Malik was born.

ELINORE: Oh, my God. How?

DEBORAH: Car accident. [*At* MICHAEL.] A drunk driver.

MICHAEL: Connor's life was just one fucking disaster after another. [*Pause.*] I won't let you ruin his son's life.

DEBORAH: Ruin! How could I ruin Malik's life? He'd have every opportunity—he'd have two loving parents—and siblings someday.

MICHAEL: You've got two wombs between you—make your own damn baby. For the right price, I'm sure you can find some guy to jerk off in a cup.

ELINORE: Michael...

MICHAEL: That's what they do! It's a fucking industry—part of the lesbian economy.

DEBORAH: You are so fucking ignorant.

MICHAEL: Nice language for a mom-to-be. Any kid would be rolling the dice with you for a mother.

ELINORE: You'd make a wonderful mother, Deborah. It's just that Malik—well, he doesn't really *belong* to us. [*She looks at* DEBORAH *meaningfully.*] Does he.

DEBORAH: So where's he supposed to go? His mother's dead, Simone's a fucking bitch...

MICHAEL: I'm sure she shares the same high opinion of you.

DEBORAH: I'm not the one who called Children's Services, Mike.

ELINORE: Who did?

DEBORAH: [*Pause.*] Simone.

MICHAEL: You're lying.

DEBORAH: I'm not—I hired a lawyer and a private investigator. They talked to the neighbors, the case worker. It had to be her! Simone reported Connor for abuse.

ELINORE: No!

MICHAEL: No way. No fucking way! Connor would never hurt Malik. Not after everything he went through as a kid...

DEBORAH: Right. So obviously Simone is lying. Either the abuse never happened, or the abuser was someone else in that household.

ELINORE: Simone...

MICHAEL: This is ridiculous—why would she call and report herself?

DEBORAH: How should I know? Maybe she was jealous of Connor's relationship with his son. Maybe she just wanted Malik out of the way. All I know is, Malik needs a new family.

MICHAEL: That's right—a *family*, not a freak show.

DEBORAH: What is it with you? Most drunks slur their speech and pass out. You turn into a raving right-wing homophobe.

MICHAEL: I'm not afraid of you. I'm afraid of what you'd do to Connor's boy.

DEBORAH: Because I'm a lesbian!

MICHAEL: Because you're a liberal light-weight who doesn't know the first thing about race! You only want a black kid to complete your little rainbow coalition.

DEBORAH: Malik's a child—not a color. I'd only see him as my son.

MICHAEL: Race isn't just about color—there's his culture to consider. What do you know about black people—the way they live, the things they believe?

DEBORAH: Allie and I have plenty of black friends—

MICHAEL: [*Groans.*] Oh, God. You're embarrassing, you know that?

DEBORAH: Get used to us, Michael. We're not going to die out and we're not going to disappear. In fact, we're the future…

MICHAEL: Then the whole fucking country's doomed.

DEBORAH: [*She struggles against her rising hysteria.*] Go on and drink yourself into oblivion. The world could use one less asshole. What have you ever contributed—huh? What have you ever made or given to the world? At least Connor was an artist—at least he turned his pain into something else instead of looking for pity at the bottom of a bottle. You think just 'cause you're straight, you've got a right to reproduce? They ought to tie *your* tubes! It's people like you who are the problem. You ruin everything—everything!

MICHAEL: That's right—people like me. MANKIND—that's what you're thinking, right? What do you know about raising a son? You'd probably just punish the kid for being male.

DEBORAH: There's no hate in our home, Michael. [*The tears she has been fighting pour forth.*] Allie and I—we'd have nothing but love for that child…

ELINORE: [*Softly, to herself.*] It takes more than love.

DEBORAH: What?

ELINORE: [*To* MICHAEL.] You think I'm a monster for reversing the adoption. But you don't know what it's like raising a child that everyone knows isn't your own. The stares, the whispers, the insults, the jokes…you're supposed to be his mother, but you can't even do simple things, like comb his hair! You feel like such a failure. It wounds you deep inside.

MICHAEL: [*Callous.*] This isn't about you. [*To* DEBORAH.] Or you. It's about what's best for Malik.

ELINORE: I tried. God knows I tried... [*Starts to weep and fumbles in her purse for a bottle of pills.* DEBORAH *frowns as* ELINORE *downs a pill without water, but nonetheless moves over to her mother and tries to comfort her. There is a knock at the door.* "Room Service." DEBORAH *looks at* MICHAEL, *and he pulls himself up to answer the door. He accepts the tray of food, sets it on the table, and generously tips the (black) bellboy.*]

MICHAEL: I'll see you later. [*He grabs his suit jacket and puts it back on.*]

DEBORAH: Where are you going?

MICHAEL: Out. [*Opens the door and exits.* ELINORE *dissolves in tears.* DEBORAH *rocks her soothingly. Lights down.*]

# ACT I

## Scene 4

[*A dimly lit lounge; red spotlights give the place a hip and/or hell-like atmosphere. Al Green is playing on the stereo. A few patrons stand at the bar, but most of the booths are empty.* MICHAEL *sits in one booth, drinking; he appears anxious. He is obviously waiting for someone. The door opens, bells jangle, and* SIMONE *stands in the doorway, squinting in the dim light. She spots Michael and makes her way over to the booth.*]

MICHAEL: Hey. [*He starts to rise but she ignores the gesture and slides into the booth.*] Thanks for coming.

SIMONE: Thank *you*. I needed an excuse to get out of there.

MICHAEL: [*Hails the waitress.*] What'll you have?

SIMONE: [*Sighs heavily.*] Gin and tonic.

MICHAEL: [*To waitress.*] Gin and tonic for the lady, and a refill for me. [*Pause, as waitress withdraws.*] It's your place. Can't you just ask them to leave?

SIMONE: I could. But then I'd be stuck there alone, which might be worse than having a house full of Marva's church "family."

MICHAEL: You two are pretty close, huh?

SIMONE: [*Hesitates.*] Connor wanted her in his life. It wasn't really up to me.

MICHAEL: And if it were?

SIMONE: [*Their drinks arrive.*] If your mother chose drugs over you, how would you feel?

MICHAEL: I'd probably hate her guts.

SIMONE: Me, too. But Connor's therapist thought it might help if he reconnected with his birth mother. He'd had her name for years—it was on his birth certificate—but they only got in touch a few months ago.

MICHAEL: Around the same time as his conversion?

SIMONE: [*She partially nods.*] It wasn't a complete conversion. Connor adopted—*adapted* aspects of the faith that appealed to him. The rituals, the act of submission. He was…searching, I guess.

MICHAEL: For roots?

SIMONE: Structure. Order. A sense of purpose and belonging. Connor wanted to make peace with the past.

MICHAEL: So…can you tell me what happened? [*Pause.*] Deb says you called Children's Services.

SIMONE: And you believe her?

MICHAEL: I don't know what to believe.

SIMONE: So that's why you're here? To interrogate me?

MICHAEL: Relax, Simone. I'm on your side. I'm not about to let Deb get her hands on Malik.

SIMONE: [*Pause; she relents, accepting his support.*] She's serious?

MICHAEL: I'm afraid so.

SIMONE: She's got a hell of a lot of nerve.

MICHAEL: It runs in the family. [*Pause.*] Is she lying about the abuse?

SIMONE: [*Pause.*] Children's Services was investigating us. Someone—I don't know who—said they suspected Malik was being abused.

MICHAEL: By Connor.

SIMONE: They questioned both of us. It was awful. Just awful. [*She covers her face with her hands.*]

MICHAEL: Did they find any proof?

SIMONE: Of course not! But by the time they figured that out…it was too late.

MICHAEL: It was you who found him? [SIMONE *nods silently.*] Christ…I'm sorry, Simone. For everything. No one should have to deal with what you're going through.

SIMONE: Save your sympathy for Connor. He's the one who suffered the most.

MICHAEL: What about Malik?

SIMONE: What about him?

MICHAEL: What happens now?

SIMONE: I don't know. ACS put him in a temporary foster home. They're trying to determine who should be given legal custody.

MICHAEL: You're at the top of their list, right? I mean, you and Connor were engaged to be married.

SIMONE: That doesn't mean anything. I'm not a blood relative.

MICHAEL: Who is?

SIMONE: [*Laughs derisively, and takes a sip of her drink.*] Marva.

MICHAEL: Damn. You got to be kidding me. She walks out on Connor thirty years ago, and now she's first in line to take care of his kid?

SIMONE: She says she wants us to be a family. She'd be willing to share custody, I think.

MICHAEL: And you'd do that? She was an addict for Christ's sake.

SIMONE: She's been clean for more than ten years. And everyone deserves a second chance. That's what Connor believed. He wanted her in his life—in Malik's life. What choice do I have? If I fight her and lose, I'll never see Malik again.

MICHAEL: Deb's serious, Simone. You better get a good lawyer. And tell Marva to watch her back. There's a private investigator, too.

SIMONE: Snooping around trying to dig up dirt, huh? To prove we're unfit mothers...well, maybe we are. She makes my skin crawl, that woman.

MICHAEL: Marva? She looked pretty torn up at the funeral.

SIMONE: She'd never pass up that role—all eyes on the grieving mother.

MICHAEL: It was an act?

SIMONE: Who knows. Sometimes I think she's for real, and other times it seems like all she cares about is what the people at that damn church think of her. "Sister Marva"—ha! Saint Marva, more like. She's got all those folks thinking SHE'S the victim here. [Pause.] You certainly didn't help matters any.

MICHAEL: Me? What did I do?

SIMONE: You were drunk, Michael...it was the perfect opportunity to expose Marva, and instead you wound up confirming what all those black folks already think about whites.

MICHAEL: That we can't hold our liquor?

SIMONE: That you don't know how to act right. Not even at a funeral. Those church folks took one look at you and gave Marva all their sympathy.

MICHAEL: I'm sorry we made a scene, but...I was upset! You don't know what it's like, being part of that family.

SIMONE: I know what it did to Connor.

MICHAEL: Yeah, well...sometimes I think Connor was the lucky one. [*Simone regards him icily.*] I don't mean that—I know what he went through. It's just that...I always kind of envied Connor. He beat the odds, you know. He broke free from the Fitzgerald clan, he made something of himself. He didn't turn into a statistic.

SIMONE: Didn't he?

MICHAEL: It was his choice, Simone. You got to respect that.

SIMONE: Connor killed himself because he thought he *had* no choice, Michael. They pushed him to his limit and he snapped. Why the fuck should I respect that?

MICHAEL: You have every right to be angry, Simone. But I can't change what happened thirty years ago. If it had been up to me…I was just a kid then.

SIMONE: I'm not blaming you, Michael. But I'm not in the mood for any philosophical rambling about the nobility of suicide. There's no way to make this look good.

MICHAEL: No, I guess you're right. [*There is an awkward pause. Michael wants to reach out to her, but she is distant.*] I talked to him just a couple of weeks ago, you know. He sounded good. Really good. He was psyched about that book you two were collaborating on.

SIMONE: Connor had good days and bad days. When he was painting, he was fine. Ecstatic, even. He'd be sitting in his studio, humming, singing, laughing to himself. And then some days I'd go in there and he'd just be staring out the window. No smiles, no songs. Just this hollow kind of pain seeping out of him. I—I didn't always know what to do. But he knew he could come to me. Connor taught me how to listen and not judge. He taught me how to forgive even the most hateful people. I wish he had come to me…

MICHAEL: I'm sure he wanted to, Simone. But I think Connor felt he had to protect us.

SIMONE: From what?

MICHAEL: From…his past. His ghosts.

SIMONE: He protected us, but no one protected him.

MICHAEL: Did he ever talk to you about…those years? After we gave him up?

SIMONE: He talked about it with his therapist, I think. Sometimes he'd come home from a session, and he'd be willing to talk—not for long, and he'd never really tell a complete story. He just had fragments…memories sharp as shattered glass. He tried to handle them carefully…but they cut him just the same. I kept hoping his shrink would give Connor a box—someplace to put all those jagged pieces of his past. He'd held onto them long enough. [*Pause.*] There were scars. On his body.

MICHAEL: [*Stares at her but she avoids his eyes.*] Scars?

SIMONE: Cigarette burns on his thighs. Strange keloids on his back. [*Pause.*] I can only imagine what he went through. [*She takes a sip and tries not to explode.*] And where was ACS then, huh? Where were they when Connor needed protecting?

MICHAEL: [*Drains his drink and hails the waitress for a refill.*] Deb thinks Malik can make us clean again. She calls him our "second chance."

SIMONE: What makes her think she'd do any better than your mother?

MICHAEL: Deb's a righteous dyke. She figures Dad was the problem, not Mom. Take the man out of the picture, and presto! Instant perfect family.

SIMONE: Why doesn't she do *in vitro* or something?

MICHAEL: She plans to, I think. But Malik's already here. I'm telling you—my sister's got this crazy idea about the future of families—"alternate models of parenting"—blah, blah, blah. If Deb's the future, then the human race is screwed.

SIMONE: [*Regards him for a moment.*] What makes Deb a bad parent, Michael—the fact that she's gay, or the fact that she's white?

MICHAEL: You want her to raise Malik?

SIMONE: No. But if she wanted to adopt a different black child, I wouldn't necessarily object. A good home is a good home, Michael. If the choice is gay parents or foster care…[*She shrugs.*] Most kids just want someone to love. They want to feel like they belong to somebody.

MICHAEL: Kids aren't property.

SIMONE: [*Narrows her eyes.*] Don't tell me my history, Michael. This is adoption—not the auction block.

MICHAEL: Oh yeah? This could be just a trend, Simone—a few celebrities adopt children in Africa, and all of a sudden everybody wants their very own cute black kid. What happens when those adoptions go out of style? Connor happens, that's what.

SIMONE: You think that little of your own sister?

MICHAEL: She doesn't deserve Connor's child. Motherhood is a social experiment for Deb. She only became a lesbian to get back at our dad.

SIMONE: You don't believe that.

MICHAEL: Ask her yourself. She hates his fucking guts. And mine.

SIMONE: Maybe it's not you she hates. [*Pause.*] Maybe it's the drinking.

MICHAEL: You, too, huh? Christ. I can't catch a break today.

SIMONE: You trying to end up like your dad?

MICHAEL: Maybe.

SIMONE: Connor said you told him you had a handle on it. He said you'd joined a group.

MICHAEL: Yeah, well, that was before I got the call telling me my kid brother hanged himself off the fire escape. I'll get back on the wagon when all this is over.

SIMONE: It may never be over.

[MICHAEL *shrugs and looks yearningly into his empty glass.*]

SIMONE: [*Gently.*] You're a decent guy, Michael. Connor wanted you to be happy. The others…he didn't really care about. But you—you still mattered to him.

MICHAEL: [*Fights but cannot contain his emotion.*] Oh, God, Simone…I feel like I'm rotting inside!

SIMONE: Get help, Michael. It's not too late.

MICHAEL: [*Loudly.*] It is too late! Connor's gone. I never even got a chance to say, "I'm sorry."

SIMONE: [*Forces herself to summon compassion she doesn't necessarily feel.*] There was nothing to apologize for. You said it yourself, you were just a kid.

MICHAEL: I loved him so much…you don't know what he was like back then.

SIMONE: Tell me.

MICHAEL: [*Sniffs, wipes his sleeve across his face.*] When you're a kid, you don't know what race is all about. You can tell when someone's different, but you don't know what it means…it doesn't matter until someone tells you it matters. Mom and Dad brought Connor home and he was…perfect. He almost never cried. Everything he needed, we had. Deb already had me for a little brother, so she wasn't as excited as I was. Connor was *my* baby brother. I was six years old. I'd never felt so…important. I taught him to walk, to read, to write his name. And he loved to draw—his favorite color was orange. He was mine, Simone. Connor's all I ever had…

SIMONE: How did your mother explain—

MICHAEL: [*Bitter.*] She didn't. She said we were moving to California, but Dad wasn't coming with us. She took Connor with her and went out to run some errands. She came back alone.

SIMONE: [*Incredulous.*] She must have said something.

MICHAEL: She said Connor was going to stay with Dad for a while. It wasn't until we were settled in California that she told us Connor was…gone.

SIMONE: God—what a heartless bitch.

MICHAEL: I don't know if she felt anything then, but she feels it now. She feels it now.

[*There is a long silence between them. Simone checks her watch and prepares to leave.*]

SIMONE: I should go. I don't want Marva to worry.

MICHAEL: [*Clears his throat and tries to pull himself together.*] Right, right. [*Simone rises and Michael feels something like panic.*] Simone—can I see you again? I mean, could we…keep in touch.

SIMONE: I don't know, Michael. I can't keep having this conversation. The past—it hurts too much.

MICHAEL: I know, I understand. It's just that—well, I feel closer to Connor when I'm with you. And I—I'd like to know Malik.

SIMONE: [*Regards him and softens somewhat; she tries not to be cruel.*] Malik doesn't need an uncle who's a drunk. I'm sorry, Michael, but Connor wouldn't want his son to see you this way.

MICHAEL: [*Shaken, humbled.*] I'll get help. I promise. For Connor.

SIMONE: [*Shakes her head and rests her hand on his.*] For you.

MICHAEL: I promise.

SIMONE: You've got my number. [*He nods.*] Then keep in touch.

[*She turns to go, but he grasps her hand.*]

MICHAEL: Connor told me you redeemed him. Those were his words—*she redeems me.*

SIMONE: [*Shakes her head and shakes loose his grasp.*] But I didn't save him. Did I.

[*She turns and leaves the bar. MICHAEL contemplates his empty glass, fights the urge to refill it, and finally drops his head into his hands.*]

## ACT I

### Scene 5

[*Simone returns from the bar and finds her apartment empty except for Marva and an older gentleman who are seated on the sofa, seemingly reminiscing. Though she wants to be alone, Simone's "home training" won't allow her to disappear into Connor's studio, which is where she wants to be. The apartment is funky, youthful, "shabby chic"—Connor's large, colorful paintings adorn the walls, and the furniture is stylish yet "kid friendly"—there are some toys tucked away in corners, on shelves, etc.*]

MARVA: [*Laughs and acts coquettish, despite the circumstances. She and the man seem to have history. At the sound of Simone's key in the door, Marva spins around, but doesn't rise. Her irritation/surprise at being interrupted quickly turns to motherly concern.*] At last! We were starting to worry about you.

SIMONE: [*Dismayed to find her apartment isn't empty.*] Sorry. I guess I should have called. [*They both look at her, expectantly.*] I met a friend and then took a walk.

MARVA: In this weather? [*Gets up from the sofa and approaches Simone, arms open wide. She either doesn't see or disregards Simone's disdain.*] Come here, baby. [*She folds a stiff Simone in her arms.*] I know just how you feel. You got to just let it out…let it out and give it up to God. [*She grips Simone's arms and looks her dead in the face.*] Only our Heavenly Father can ease a sorrow this deep. Why, me and Deacon Barlow were praying for Connor just a moment ago. He's in a better place now.

BARLOW: [*Rises from the sofa; he is deferential, solemn now.*] Good evening.

SIMONE: [*Pulls herself away from Marva. To Barlow.*] Good evening. [*Removes her coat and tries to exit gracefully.*] I guess I am a bit damp. If you don't mind, I think I'll turn in for the night. It's been a long day. [*She waits by the door, hoping they'll leave.*]

MARVA: [*Marva fails to take the hint.*] Don't I know it. I'm exhausted! I was going to ask the deacon to see me home, but I think I'd better stay here with you tonight. [*Marva's dramatic gestures and Simone's true feelings seem transparent to Deacon Barlow. He offers Simone a sympathetic smile and moves closer to the door, as if to leave.*]

BARLOW: I guess I'll be moving on then.

MARVA: But Simone just got here! I want you two to get to know each other. [*She grabs Barlow and drags him closer to Simone.*] Take a good look at him—don't be shy.

BARLOW: Marva—

MARVA: Hush, now! Don't say another word. [*To Simone.*] Well?

SIMONE: [*Perplexed, annoyed.*] Marva, I really am tired…

BARLOW: Leave her be, now. We can talk another time.

MARVA: Nonsense! She ain't too tired to meet the man who would have been her father-in-law. [*Simone's mouth falls open, and Marva beams.*] Can't you see the resemblance? This here is Deacon John Barlow—or Johnnie, as I used to call him back in the day. Connor's father.

BARLOW: Pleased to meet you, Miss, though I sure do wish the circumstances could have been different.

SIMONE: [*Remembers herself and takes his proffered hand. She is scanning his face for proof that he is related to Connor.*] I—I didn't know…[*She turns to Marva.*] Did Connor—?

MARVA: They only talked on the phone a couple of times. I meant for all of us to get together, but…well, I waited too long, I guess. [*She sniffs, and Barlow puts a hand on her shoulder.*]

BARLOW: You can't keep blaming yourself, Marva. What's done is done.

[*The phone rings and before Simone can move to answer it, Marva jumps to life.*]

MARVA: That'll be Sister Bernice. I asked her to call me as soon as she got in. Sit down, you two, sit down—I'll be right back. [*She exits, and we hear her talking animatedly on the phone, switching from the role of grieving mother to catty gossip.*]

SIMONE: [*Stands awkwardly in her own home, unsure what to say or do. Barlow is just as uncomfortable. He stands holding his hat; Simone is still holding her coat.*] So.

BARLOW: I'm awfully sorry, Miss. For your loss, and…for meeting this way. Marva—she never did have good timing. [*An awkward pause.*] Are your folks in town?

SIMONE: [*Distracted—she is fighting the urge to scrutinize him for proof that he is Connor's biological father.*] Hm?

BARLOW: Your kinfolk—are they close by?

SIMONE: My parents live in Westchester, but they're on a cruise right now. I decided to wait and tell them once they get back.

BARLOW: [*Surprised at her nonchalance.*] Wouldn't you rather have them here with you? It's a difficult time to be alone.

SIMONE: [*Shrugs and tries to drop another hint.*] I can't remember the last time I was alone. [*Slight pause.*] My parents never really approved of Connor—[*dryly*] my mother was hoping I'd bring home a stockbroker. [*Her true emotion breaks through for a moment.*] There's nothing they could do, anyway.

BARLOW: Still…[*He glances offstage to where Marva is.*] …it might be comforting to have your *own* kin nearby.

SIMONE: Death isn't supposed to be comfortable. Not for the ones left behind. [*Another awkward pause; Simone's fatigue, grief, and resentment begin to get the better of her. Her tone becomes caustic, snide.*] You and Marva must go way back.

BARLOW: We have…history, yes.

SIMONE: [*Cruelly.*] I hear Marva was a real party girl back in the day. A guaranteed good time.

BARLOW: [*Looks down at his hat and smiles slightly, shaming Simone.*] You don't have to like me, Miss. When I think back on that time in my life, I don't much like myself.

SIMONE: [*Relents somewhat.*] You were at the funeral?

BARLOW: Yes. It was a fine service.

SIMONE: Connor never mentioned you.

BARLOW: Well, Marva only just put us in touch. I didn't know he'd been looking. If I'd known…[*He appeals to her, moves closer, but she remains unmoved.*] He seems like a person I'd like to have met. I used to draw a little when I was in the service. Just doodling, really. Never had no formal training. And you're an artist, too, I hear. A writer?

SIMONE: Yes.

BARLOW: I thought your eulogy was beautiful. A fine tribute to a fine young man.

SIMONE: [*Moves towards the sofa and deposits her coat*.] It was the least I could do. Words are all I can give Connor now.

BARLOW: Situations like these, it's easy to think—to wonder whether something could have been done differently…but you can't blame yourself.

SIMONE: I guess absolution comes easy for some.

BARLOW: I think it's easier to forgive others than to forgive yourself.

SIMONE: [From offstage we hear a shriek of laughter from Marva, who is still on the phone.] It wasn't that hard for Marva.

BARLOW: [*He seems shamed by Marva's hilarity, yet determined to defend her.*] Some folks just can't stand thinking about the past—it hurts too much. And what's done is done. God grants us the serenity to accept the things we cannot change… [*Pause; he can tell Simone is hardening against him as she has hardened against Marva.*] Marva was young then. Alone. I was just back from Nam—not much use to anybody, including myself. She did what she thought was best.

SIMONE: Best for Connor—or for herself?

BARLOW: Marva wanted to give her baby boy a better life. Even today, a black boy in this city doesn't stand much of a chance.

Between the guns and the gangs, trigger happy police…Rich white family out in Connecticut—she couldn't have known it would turn out this way. [*Pause; he tries to gauge her capacity for compassion.*] Do you have children?

SIMONE: No. Do you?

BARLOW: My wife is a good woman, and we've been blessed in many ways, but the Lord didn't see fit to give us children.

SIMONE: [*Loses some of her restraint.*] Then why didn't you take Connor? After the adoption fell through—you could have raised him yourself!

BARLOW: It took a few years, but once I finally got clean—stopped drinking, shooting up—I lost touch with Marva. We'd never really been close. We were more what you would call—occasional friends.

SIMONE: Fuck buddies.

BARLOW: I guess that's fair. We were intimate in that way, but we weren't close. [*Pause.*] I always blamed myself for what happened to her.

SIMONE: She didn't have to spread her legs. She could have been a "good girl"—a God-fearing woman, like she is now.

BARLOW: I meant the drugs. Marva was a simple country girl. She didn't know many people in the city, and she started moving with the wrong crowd—people I introduced her to…

SIMONE: Nothing you say will change what she did.

BARLOW: No, we can't undo the past. But the living have more use for sympathy than the dead.

SIMONE: That's mighty Christian of you.

BARLOW: I know a thing or two about anger. I used to be angry at the world.

SIMONE: Until you found God?

BARLOW: Until I took responsibility for my life—stopped blaming the Man, the dope.

SIMONE: Why are you giving me a lecture on responsibility?

BARLOW: [*Pause.*] Connor had a boy.

SIMONE: Yes.

BARLOW: Marva says you're going to raise him together.

SIMONE: She's his only blood relative. She'll get custody. Unless you want to jump into the fray.

BARLOW: I'd love nothing more than a grandson. But I'm in no position to raise a child—not at my age. [*Pause.*] Seems to me you'd be the best candidate.

SIMONE: He isn't mine.

BARLOW: He belonged to the man you loved. The man you were going to marry.

SIMONE: [*Turns away; shamed.*] Black boys don't stand a chance in this city—that's what you just said, right?

BARLOW: What I meant was…they face particular challenges.

SIMONE: Right. And most don't make it.

BARLOW: We lose too many to the streets. Many live, but in a state of limbo—no longer boys, yet not quite men. But some—some do reach manhood.

SIMONE: A boy needs a man in his life, in his home. I have nothing to offer a son.

BARLOW: My father wasn't there for me.

SIMONE: And you weren't there for Connor.

BARLOW: No. But by the grace of our Heavenly Father, I turned my life around.

SIMONE: You beat the odds.

BARLOW: Yes.

SIMONE: You were lucky.

BARLOW: Blessed. I couldn't have done it alone. I had help.

SIMONE: Connor needed help.

BARLOW: I know. And I'm sorry, Miss. You'll never know just how sorry I am…

SIMONE: Do you believe in redemption?

BARLOW: Of course.

SIMONE: [*Desperate, impassioned.*] Then why don't *you* take Malik? Take him out of the city—give him the chance your own son never had.

BARLOW: I can't do that, Miss.

SIMONE: Why not? You're not that old! [*She becomes vicious again.*] Or are you afraid your perfect wife will discover you're not the holy man you pretend to be?

BARLOW: I don't keep secrets from my wife. She knows about Connor—and Marva. And you. [*Deflated, Simone loses her bluster. He speaks to her gently.*] You're not as hard as you pretend to be. You loved Connor. And you have every right to be mad at the folks who let him down. But don't let his boy suffer—he's not the one who should be punished for all this.

SIMONE: [*Weakly.*] What do you want me to do?

BARLOW: I think, together, we could convince Marva to step aside. If you wanted sole custody, she'd give it to you.

SIMONE: She said that?

BARLOW: Not in so many words…but Marva's no spring chicken. She wants to do what's right, but she can't raise that child alone. And you don't need her moving in here. You and the boy—you need to start your own life together.

SIMONE: [*Simone reaches for one of the toys strewn about the apartment and fingers it thoughtfully.*] No one's asked Malik what *he* wants.

BARLOW: The child's too young to know his own mind. I'm sure none of this makes any sense to him. The boy just wants to come home.

[*They stand together in silence until Marva enters from offstage.*]

MARVA: That Bernice—I love her to pieces, but she can talk a blue streak! [*She regards them for a moment, trying to gauge what has happened in her absence.*] How about a nice hot cup of coffee?

SIMONE: I'll get it. [*She hastens to leave the room.*]

MARVA: No, no—I insist. I'll be the hostess, and you be the guest. You two just make yourselves comfortable…

BARLOW: Actually, Marva, I think it's time I went home.

MARVA: Already? But Simone just got here.

BARLOW: Well, we've had a chance to get acquainted. And I'm hoping we'll have a chance to talk some more one day. [*He asks Simone with his eyes, and she nods silently.*] I think maybe you two should sit down and talk about the boy.

MARVA: Connor?

SIMONE: Malik.

MARVA: We've got to go down there first thing tomorrow morning. [*Simone looks surprised.*] The social worker called while you were out. There's a preliminary hearing at nine o'clock.

BARLOW: Marva, why don't you walk out with me? I'd like to speak with you in private. [*Marva darts her eyes at Simone; she is suddenly suspicious of them both.*] It'll just take a moment. [*He gestures towards the door. She hesitates, then relaxes, smiles, and opens it for him.*]

MARVA: Sure, Johnnie. Whatever you say. [*They exit, with Barlow nodding to Simone before he leaves. Once they are gone, Simone stands alone and awkward in the apartment. She tries to avoid it, but is drawn to the fire escape. She is standing by the window, transfixed, when Marva reenters.*] So, you've made up your mind, huh?

SIMONE: Made up my mind? About what?

MARVA: To get sole custody of Malik. I thought we agreed to work together—as a family.

SIMONE: I haven't decided anything, Marva. Your deacon just suggested we talk about it some more.

MARVA: So? What have you got to say?

SIMONE: [*Flustered, too tired for a hostile confrontation.*] I don't know! He said you were too—

MARVA: What? Too old? I'll have you know I am in the prime of my life, young lady!

SIMONE: [*Sinks onto the sofa, holding her head.*] Marva, please. It's been such a difficult day…I don't want to fight with you.

MARVA: [*Tries to stem her anger, and eventually sits on the sofa, though not too close to Simone.*] You never said you wanted to raise him by yourself.

SIMONE: We don't even know if it's possible, do we? You've got the strongest claim on Malik.

MARVA: [*Frowns less, somewhat mollified.*] He already thinks of you as his mama.

SIMONE: [*Flinches.*] No matter what happens at the hearing tomorrow, Malik will always be Connor's child. And your grandchild.

MARVA: He's your stepchild.

SIMONE: [*Wearily.*] We weren't married, Marva.

MARVA: You practically were…you lived together, you worked together, you were raising Malik together. You're the only mother he knows.

SIMONE: [*Pause.*] I don't know if I can do it alone.

MARVA: [*She reaches a hand across the sofa to squeeze Simone's knee.*] You won't be alone.

SIMONE: [*Hesitates, then dares to be honest.*] I never wanted children. Not until I met Connor. Not until I saw how much he loved that little boy.

MARVA: Contrary to what some folks think, we ain't all cut from the same cloth. Some women got it in 'em, some don't.

SIMONE: [*Cautiously.*] Which kind of woman were you?

MARVA: [*Pause; her chin goes up instinctively, a reflex reaction she has learned over time.*] I wanted my baby. Folks think if you put your baby up for adoption, it's 'cause you don't want him. But that ain't true. Not for me, anyhow. I always wanted my baby.

SIMONE: Then why did you give him away?

MARVA: [*Shrugs simply.*] I couldn't take care of him. Not the way I wanted. Not like how he deserved.

SIMONE: You gave Connor away and he still never had the childhood he deserved. [*Pause.*] It might have been kinder to have had an abortion.

MARVA: [*Shocked.*] I told you already—I wanted my baby! I wanted him alive in this world. I wanted him to have a chance. Look! [*She gestures at the paintings on the walls.*] Look at what my boy did with his life.

SIMONE: Connor used to tell me he was grateful…he said the universe had a plan for his life, and so there were no mistakes, no sins to be forgiven. He said we never would have met if you'd raised him on your own.

MARVA: [*Tearful.*] He was an angel, my boy. He wouldn't even let me say, "I'm sorry."

SIMONE: Were you?

MARVA: Sorry? I was sick—sick, you hear! After I gave my baby away I had a hole inside of me that nothing could fill. And I tried…for years I put every kind of nastiness inside my body. But nothing could make me whole.

SIMONE: Not even God?

MARVA: [*Pause.*] The first time I felt whole again was when Connor came back. My baby found me. And he wasn't angry…he had forgiven me.

SIMONE: Your deacon said it's easier to forgive others than to forgive yourself. You think that's what happened to Connor?

MARVA: You knew him better—longer—than me. What do you think?

SIMONE: I don't know. I keep thinking about it—wondering if it was one thing or a combination of things all at once…if they had taken Malik but I had kept his ring, would Connor still be alive? I wasn't going to leave him…no matter what, I never would have left him alone…[*She covers her face with her hands and weeps.*]

MARVA: [*Hesitates; she watches Simone for a moment, struggling to overcome her resistance to sympathize with the woman who rejected her son. Finally, she moves closer to Simone and embraces her.*] Shhh. Connor's home now, baby. He ain't gon' suffer no more. [*Simone sobs louder; lights down.*]

# ACT I

## Scene 6

[*Ruth's office at the literary agency. Her desk is crowded with books and stacks of papers, a computer. On the wall are framed photographs—head shots—of her clients. Simone is seated in one of the plush leather chairs that face Ruth's desk; she is alternately sullen, fidgety, terse. Ruth is trying to be sensitive, but her impulse is clearly to conduct business as usual. Their conversation is interrupted by the frequent ringing of the phone, and Ruth clearly resists the urge to check emails on her computer screen.*]

RUTH: So? [*Simone looks flat, unresponsive.*] How did it go?

SIMONE: We won't know until tomorrow. The judge just wanted to hear from all of the "interested parties."

RUTH: Well, that's good. It'll all be over soon, then. [*Simone glares at her. Ruth clears her throat and tries a more delicate tone.*] You know, I wasn't entirely sure you were interested. [*Simone raises an eyebrow.*] It's just that for as long as I've known you, you've always said that you didn't want to be a mother. Ever.

SIMONE: [*Simone looks away.*] It's a woman's prerogative to change her mind.

RUTH: Of course, of course! And under the circumstances, I can hardly blame you for feeling an obligation to that poor child…

SIMONE: Don't call him that.

RUTH: What?

SIMONE: That "poor child" is named Malik.

RUTH: I know, dear. I only meant to suggest that you're under a tremendous amount of pressure right now…there's a certain—expectation—that isn't, well, that isn't entirely *reasonable*.

SIMONE: What are you talking about, Ruth?

RUTH: Well, you've just lost the man you love under… extraordinarily difficult circumstances. It isn't really fair for them to

36

expect you to look after his child. [*She pauses strategically to gauge Simone's feelings.*] Is it? After all, you're still grieving.

SIMONE: [*Suddenly seems uncertain.*] You think I should give him up?

RUTH: I think you deserve time to heal. Being a mother myself, I feel I have an obligation to be honest with you, my dear. It isn't easy. Parenting is such hard work, especially when you're on your own.

SIMONE: I think I could manage, if I had help.

RUTH: And who would help you, Simone? Connor's mother? Could you really trust her around a child?

SIMONE: She's not an addict any more, Ruth.

RUTH: Still…old habits die hard. And your own parents— how would they feel about you raising Connor's son?

SIMONE: Who cares what they think!

RUTH: Now, Simone. I realize this is a difficult time for you, but you've got to be realistic about this. Have you talked to your mother since…

SIMONE: No.

RUTH: Do you think that's wise, dear?

SIMONE: She and my father are cruising the Hawaiian Islands—you know that. They'll be back next week.

RUTH: Then I suggest you wait and not make any hasty decisions until you've had a chance to talk it over. A mother's counsel is priceless.

SIMONE: I don't need to wait—I already know what she'll say.

RUTH: Your mother has always struck me as a remarkably savvy woman, Simone. She knows a thing or two about the ways of the world. She's cultured—a true sophisticate.

SIMONE: [*Sarcastic.*] Are you her agent, or mine?

RUTH: Yours, of course. I just hate to see you turning away from the person who loves you best.

SIMONE: The person who loved me best is dead. [*Pause.*] Enough already! I didn't come here for therapy, Ruth. When you said we needed to talk, I assumed it had something to do with work.

RUTH: Yes, of course. Let's move on. I've had a call from Christine—the editor at Meadow Press.

SIMONE: What about? Are the final proofs ready?

RUTH: Not quite. Christine said Connor had promised her some additional artwork—something extra for the book's end sheets.

SIMONE: I—I don't know. He never mentioned it to me. I can check his studio…

RUTH: Would you, dear? The sooner the better. We don't want to keep our editor waiting. There's really nothing we can do about this…unfortunate incident, but I think we might as well use the extra publicity to our advantage.

SIMONE: [*Deadly.*] What?

RUTH: Well, I'm sure I don't have to tell you, my dear, that suicide doesn't sell—not when you're writing for children, anyway. Fortunately, I've been able to keep the more—graphic details of Connor's death out of the papers. He was very well respected, you know, but sympathy doesn't last forever. If we time it right, the book will seem like a tribute to Connor's artistic genius—the capstone on a remarkable but, sadly, abbreviated career. [*Simone stares at Ruth with a mixture of rage and disgust. Ruth shifts in her seat, uncomfortable. Then she boldly gets up and comes around the desk. She perches on its edge and attempts sincerity.*] I don't like this any more than you do, Simone.

SIMONE: Really? You look a bit smug, Ruth. Connor's dead and you're talking about "extra publicity" and ways to capitalize off of people's grief!

RUTH: I'm simply doing my job, Simone. You hired me to protect your interests.

SIMONE: And that's what you call this? Protection?

RUTH: You may not be ready to hear this right now, but you are my client, Simone, and I have an obligation to be frank with you. This—*incident* isn't going to help your career. In fact, it could destroy it.

SIMONE: [*Springs up and confronts Ruth, who barely flinches.*] I don't give a good God damn about my *career*, Ruth!

RUTH: You may not, but I do.

SIMONE: Because I'm your meal ticket? Or are you going to tell me again how I'm... [*She feigns a simpering voice.*] ...so much more than a client to you? [*Simone storms across the office.*] This is bullshit—total bullshit!

RUTH: This is *business*, Simone. I am your agent, your advisor, your advocate, and—believe it or not—I am your friend. But my job is not to hold your hand and whisper sweet assurances in your ear. My job is to pull you through this, and that is what I intend to do. [*Slight pause.*] You've got two choices, Simone. You can either sever your association with Connor, or you can help me reconstitute him as decent human being.

SIMONE: [*Enraged.*] Connor WAS a decent human being! He doesn't need to be repackaged. Connor was a brilliant artist who—who...met a tragic end. There's nothing shameful about that.

RUTH: [*Pauses and makes an attempt at delicacy.*] A month ago you came to my office. Do you remember the conversation we had that day?

SIMONE: [*Flustered.*] No! [*Ruth looks at her pointedly.*] We talked about the book—and whether I wanted to continue writing for children.

RUTH: That's right. And you told me—again—how uncomfortable you were with the idea of becoming a mother.

SIMONE: So?

RUTH: [*Pause.*] You said there was something strange about Connor's relationship with his son...

SIMONE: [*Struggles to maintain her anger and recall the details of their conversation.*] I said it was strange to ME! To ME, Ruth—because I didn't grow up with parents who were always hugging me and kissing me and telling me how precious I was.

RUTH: In this industry, even the hint of impropriety can be costly.

SIMONE: [*Scrutinizes Ruth as the truth gradually dawns on her.*] What are you talking about?

RUTH: You said it was "unnatural," the way Connor loved that boy.

SIMONE: I said no such thing!

RUTH:  You did!  [*She gets up and returns to her seat behind the desk.*]  And when I heard that—well!  What did you expect me to do?

SIMONE:  Nothing!

RUTH:  I'm your agent, Simone.  You don't pay me to do nothing.

SIMONE:  Oh, my God... [*Rushes over to the desk, nearly grabbing Ruth.*] WHAT DID YOU DO?  [*Ruth stares at her, coldly.  Her worst fear confirmed, Simone sinks into the chair.*]

RUTH:  I think we've said enough on this subject.  No one will ever doubt your love for Connor.  But no one would blame you for choosing your writing—your career—over his child.  You've borne enough, Simone.

SIMONE:  [*Slowly gathers herself together.  As she rises to go, she is solemn, subdued.*]  You're right, Ruth.  I do need to—sever my association...with this agency, and with you.

RUTH:  Simone—I know you're upset—but can't you see...

SIMONE:  Once this book comes out, it's over.  We're through.

RUTH:  [*Rises from her desk but Simone is already exiting the office.*] Simone!

## ACT I

## Scene 7

[*The ladies restroom at the courthouse.  Deborah emerges from a stall, her eyes red from crying.  She is talking to her partner, Allie, on her cell phone.  Deborah is alone in the bathroom and uses the moment of privacy to be her true, vulnerable self.  Her demeanor changes immediately when Simone enters.*]

DEBORAH: [*On phone to Allie.*]  It's just so unfair...[*She tugs a paper towel from the dispenser and wipes her nose, eyes.  Staring into the mirror, she listens to Allie's assurances that they'll still be mothers one day.*]  I know...I know.  I just—I get so tired of having to *fight* all the time.  [*Pause; DEB listens to Allie and nods to her reflection in the mirror.* DEB *is strengthened by Allie's words and pulls herself together.*] You're right— [*Sighs and smiles weakly.*] You're always right. What would I do without you? I wish you could have been here this week. Between my brother the drunk and my pill-popping mother...you're the only one who really loves me. [*Smiles, touched by Allie's reply.*] I miss you, too. [*Pause;* DEB *sobers, sounds more like her usual self.*] Listen, don't worry about meeting me at the airport. I'll just drop my mother off and then catch a cab back to our place. No, it's better this way—Michael's flying back with us, and you know what he's like. Why add insult to injury? Losing Malik is bad enough...

SIMONE: [*Pushes open the swinging door, smiling or perhaps waving over her shoulder to Malik.* SIMONE *sees* DEB *and her expression changes instantly.*] Oh. [DEB *turns to hide her tears but* SIMONE *sees them and starts to back out the door.*] I'll find another restroom.

DEBORAH: [*To Allie, in hushed tones.*] I have to go, hon. I'll call you later. [*Closes the phone, lifts her chin and turns to face* SIMONE *before she can retreat. Bitter, but without force.*] Congratulations, Simone. You won.

SIMONE: [*Hesitates, not wanting to engage in combat once more. But Deborah's surly tone piques her.* SIMONE *steps just inside the restroom, allowing the door to close behind her.*] It wasn't a competition, Deborah.

DEBORAH: [*Scoffs.*] Of course, it was. We were the contestants and Malik was the prize. You hit the jackpot—winner takes all.

SIMONE: [*Tries to contain her rising emotion.*] See? That's why the judge denied your application for custody. You measure everything in dollars and cents. You think just because you and your partner have six-figure salaries, you've earned the right to raise a child—MY child!

DEBORAH: Malik is Connor's boy—not yours!

SIMONE: Connor was <u>my</u> lover, <u>my</u> fiancé. And the judge said Malik belongs with me.

DEBORAH: [*Turns away, her emotions also threatening to spill over. Perhaps uses the mirrors to address* SIMONE.] Sure! According to the law of the land, you're the "right and proper" guardian. But why? Because I'm a sinner and you're a saint? Because I'm white and

41

you're black? No—because you're <u>straight</u>! Even that woman—that...crack whore! Even SHE has a right to Connor's boy. [*Spins to face* SIMONE.] You really think that's fair?

SIMONE: I'm a black woman, Deborah. Don't talk to ME about what's "fair"! I have to live in this country just like you, so don't come to me looking for sympathy. I just lost the man I love and you tried to take the last piece of him away from me...

DEBORAH: I only wanted what was best for Malik!

SIMONE: [*Exasperated but tries to keep her voice down.*] Stop <u>lying</u>, Deborah! Don't you get tired of being self-righteous all the time? You're a wealthy white woman. You could have any child in the world! But you had to have MY child!

DEBORAH: Before you ever knew him, Connor was OURS, Simone. Maybe it was just for a few years, and maybe it was half a lifetime ago, but he was ours...he was one of us.

SIMONE: [*Disgusted.*] Sure—until his race became inconvenient for your mother.

DEBORAH: [*Feels the impulse to defend her mother, but falters.*] My mother— [SIMONE *stares at her expectantly.* DEB *struggles to piece together a defense. She grows bitter as she goes on.*] My mother...has made mistakes. She...had this dream of how her life was going to be. And it was naïve—she should have known there's no such thing as "domestic bliss." But you have to remember...she married a drunk! My father thought his wife was silly and frivolous, and he never stopped mocking her...

SIMONE: So adopting Connor was just a cruel joke?

DEBORAH: [*Struggles to manage her emotions about her family's history.*] No! Dad loved Connor—in fact, he doted on him. But...Dad wouldn't stop drinking, even though my mother begged him to get help. He just gave up and let our lives unravel. [*Pause. Quietly, ashamed.*] My mother struck back at him the only way she knew how. [SIMONE *shakes her head, unable to muster any sympathy.* DEB *tries once more.*] I'm not like her! I'm not!

SIMONE: <u>That's</u> what you're trying prove?

DEBORAH: [*Deflated, near tears.*] I know I could have been a good mother to that little boy. All I wanted was a chance...

SIMONE: [*Not unkindly.*] Your family had its chance. It's time for you to let go.

DEBORAH: [*Forces herself to accept the reprimand. Makes a clumsy attempt at humility.*] You know, contrary to what Michael may have told you, I am not a scheming bitch. And I'm not part of some "lesbian conspiracy" to take over the world. I'm human, Simone.

SIMONE: We're all human, Deborah.

DEBORAH: [*Shakes her head soberly.*] You don't know what it's like, being told you're not fit to love a child.

SIMONE: [*Pause. She softens somewhat towards* DEB.] How did you get to be so…certain? About motherhood.

DEBORAH: [*Reflects, but shrugs.*] I've always wanted to have kids. I've always wanted a family that was…better than the one I got.

SIMONE: No family's perfect.

DEBORAH: I don't need perfect. Just…better.

SIMONE: [*Intrigued.*] A new and improved family, huh? I guess we could all use one of those.

DEBORAH: Human beings were designed to evolve. To grow, adapt, change. [*She glances at* SIMONE *who looks a bit lost.*] When you build a family, you build hope. [SIMONE *reflects for a moment, then nods empathetically.* DEBORAH *flicks away a tear and pulls herself together before moving towards the door.*] Malik deserves all the love Connor never got as a child. You'll give him that, won't you? [*It is not really a question, but* SIMONE *does her best to reassure* DEB.]

SIMONE: Of course. [SIMONE *tentatively reaches for* DEBORAH *who braces herself for her touch. Before they make contact,* MARVA *bursts into the restroom.*]

MARVA: There you are! I was starting to think you got flushed down the toilet. [MARVA *chuckles then realizes* SIMONE *is not alone. Upon seeing* DEB, MARVA *sours instantly.*] Oh. She giving you any trouble?

SIMONE: [*Hastens to pull* MARVA *away from* DEB *who pretends to busy herself at the sink.*] No! Let's just go—the social worker said there's some paperwork I have to take care of before we can bring Malik home. [MARVA *grumbles but allows herself to be ushered out the door by* SIMONE. *Before leaving,* SIMONE *stops and glances back at* DEBORAH, *but can think of nothing more to say.* SIMONE *exits and* DEBORAH *looks at her reflection in the mirror before dissolving in tears.*]

## ACT I

### Scene 8

[*The living room of Simone and Connor's apartment. Marva enters from the kitchen, carrying a tray for serving tea. She seems pleased and hums to herself. She places the tray on the coffee table, then sits on the sofa and begins arranging the cups, fussing as she waits for Simone. Eventually Simone enters from a bedroom offstage. She looks weary, yet satisfied.*]

MARVA: [*Turns on the sofa and looks at Simone expectantly.*] How is he?

SIMONE: Fast asleep. We didn't even get to the end of the story. [*She smiles to herself and sits in an armchair next to the sofa.*]

MARVA: [*Beams, and begins making a cup of tea for Simone.*] There'll be plenty of time for fairy tales, now that Malik's home for good. Milk?

SIMONE: [*Nods.*] Please. It's hard to believe there's really going to be a happy ending to this story.

MARVA: [*Chuckles as she passes the cup to Simone.*] Did you see the look on that judge's face when that white girl stood up in court? I knew right then and there Malik was coming home with us!

SIMONE: [*Sips her tea and looks thoughtful.*] I thought you of all people would have some sympathy for Deborah.

MARVA: Me! Why should *I* feel sorry for *her*? Skinny, rich bitch, tossing her blond hair all around the court room so folks won't think she's...you know, *funny*.

SIMONE: She's not "funny," Marva—Deborah's gay.

MARVA: Bold as any man, that one.

SIMONE: Is it so hard for you to believe she wanted Malik?

MARVA: Sure she wanted him—who wouldn't? It's all the rage now. White women tearing all over the planet, snatching up other mothers' babies. They go to China, Guatemala—and you know they just love to save those poor starving children over in Africa. Makes me sick. Then they come back home and hire a black or brown nanny to take care of their own kids! It's a mess. But Judge Evers wasn't having none of that! No, sir. He knows black children belong with black families.

SIMONE: That's not how you felt thirty years ago.

MARVA: My son was still alive thirty years ago.

SIMONE: [*Pause.*] What if there aren't enough black families to go around? [*Marva simply shrugs and sips her tea.*] Come on, Marva. After all that Connor went through, you can't honestly believe foster care is better than adoption.

MARVA: It would've been different if she was married—at least then there'd be a man in the house. God didn't intend for children to live that way—it's unnatural.

SIMONE: [*Bristles at the word and sets down her tea cup.*] I'm not Malik's natural mother. And there won't be a man in this house.

MARVA: No, but you're black—and Malik knows you. He loves you.

SIMONE: Because I'm black?

MARVA: Because you take care of him! You dress him, you feed him, you tuck him in at night.

SIMONE: Deborah could have done all of those things, Marva. [*Marva opens her mouth to object, then changes her mind.*] In an ideal world, all children would be raised by two loving parents. In the real world, we've got to do the best we can.

MARVA: That's right! And Judge Evers said YOU were the best parent for Malik.

SIMONE: Thank you, Marva.

MARVA: For what?

SIMONE: For supporting my application for custody. It wouldn't have happened without you.

MARVA: I just did what Connor would have wanted me to do. Everything's going to be alright now. [*She smiles at Simone, but the younger woman averts her gaze. The doorbell rings, and both women stir, surprised.*] You expecting company?

SIMONE: No. Are you? [*Marva shakes her head, and Simone goes to answer the door. She peers through the peephole and groans.*] Oh, God…It's my mother. [*Marva immediately begins straightening herself and the pillows on the sofa. She seems unsure whether to sit or stand. Simone takes a deep breath and opens the door.*] Mom! You're back.

IRENE: Oh, Simone. [*She kisses Simone on both cheeks before embracing her for a long moment. Simone, surprised, tolerates the embrace. Then she steps back to allow her mother to enter the apartment. Irene is polished, sophisticated. She intends to be sympathetic, but cannot hide her disdain for the artsy apartment and Simone's "common" guest. Marva rises and nearly curtsies as Irene approaches.*]

SIMONE: Mom, this is Marva—Connor's mother.

MARVA: [*Nervous but amiable.*] It's so nice to finally meet you. Now I know where Simone gets her good looks from. You two could be sisters!

IRENE: [*Smiles politely but quickly withdraws the hand Marva has seized.*] I'm sorry, you are—

SIMONE: Marva is Connor's birth mother. They reconnected a few months ago.

IRENE: I see. Well, I'm very sorry for your loss, Mrs.—

MARVA: Just call me Marva—no need to be formal when we're practically family! [*Irene, icy, freezes Marva's warm smile.*]

SIMONE: Wait a minute—you know about Connor?

IRENE: [*Impatient.*] Of course, I know. Did you really think you could keep something like this from me? [*Softens somewhat.*] I'm your mother, Simone.

SIMONE: [*Slightly ashamed.*] You were…away. I didn't see any point in ruining your vacation. Besides, [*She moves closer to Marva.*] Marva was here with me.

MARVA: I just tried to make myself useful. [*She puts her arm around Simone.*] Simone's been so strong.

IRENE: [*Clearly nonplussed by Marva's budding relationship with her daughter.*] You should have called. No matter where I was, I would have come.

MARVA: [*Sensing the tension between mother and daughter.*] We were just having some tea. Why don't I boil some more water…

IRENE: [*Turns hastily to Marva to preempt Simone.*] That would be lovely, Marva, thank you. [*Marva smiles nervously and rushes offstage. Irene waits until she is gone, then turns to Simone. She tries to soften, but her manner is still rather severe.*] So.

SIMONE: [*Sinks onto the sofa.*] So.

IRENE: [*Hesitates, then approaches the sofa and sits on its edge.*] How are you?

SIMONE: Fine. How was your cruise?

IRENE: Simone, please. Don't toy with me. Your father and I—we'd both like you to come stay with us for a while.

SIMONE: I can't.

IRENE: Why not? Surely you don't intend to stay here…[*She gestures towards the window and fire escape.*]

SIMONE: This is my home. Of course, I plan to stay here. Besides…Malik needs to stay put for a while. He's been through a lot these past few weeks, and he doesn't need any more upheaval.

IRENE: Malik?

SIMONE: [*Annoyed.*] Connor's son?

IRENE: I know who he is, Simone. I just don't see why you can't leave him with Marva and come stay with us for a while. Not forever—just until…

SIMONE: Until what, Mom?

IRENE: [*Pauses, collects herself, and tries another tack.*] What happened to Connor was…terrible. And the fact that you found him—well, that makes it doubly traumatic.

SIMONE: [*Sits back and scrutinizes her mother.*] How do you know all this?

IRENE: What?

SIMONE: [*Rises and stands over her mother.*] Who told you what happened to Connor?

IRENE: [*Falters.*] A friend of mine saw the obituary in the paper...

SIMONE: How did you know I was the one who found him? That wasn't in the papers.

IRENE: [*Rises and backs away from her daughter.*] Simone—please—I didn't come here for a confrontation...

MARVA: [*Enters and reaches for the tray on the table between them.*] The tea's almost ready. I'll just take this...

SIMONE: Don't bother, Marva. [*Simone goes over to the door.*] My mother won't be staying.

MARVA: Oh. [*She stands awkwardly beside Irene.*]

IRENE: I'm not going anywhere, Simone, until you tell me what's going on.

SIMONE: Why? You already have all the facts. Ruth called you, didn't she? She thinks you deserve a medal—as far as she's concerned, you're Mother of the Year!

IRENE: And I suppose you told her I was some kind of monster!

SIMONE: I told her that with your shining example, I could have postponed motherhood indefinitely.

IRENE: [*As if to a servant.*] Marva, would you excuse us for a moment. I'd like to speak privately with my daughter.

SIMONE: Not tonight, Mom. [*She swings open the door and is stunned to see Elinore standing uncertainly in the hallway.*]

ELINORE: Oh! [*Timidly.*] Hello. [*All three women inside the apartment stare at her, amazed.*] Have I come at a bad time? I would have called, but Michael wouldn't give me your number. I'm not here to harass you, I just—

SIMONE: [*Wearily.*] What do you want, Elinore? The judge made his decision. You have to abide by his ruling.

ELINORE: I know, I do—I mean, I will. It's just that...well, we're leaving tomorrow morning, and I—I never got a chance to see Malik.

MARVA: [*Pushes past Irene and approaches the door.*] You got no business coming here!

SIMONE: [*Gently pushes Marva back.*] Elinore, Malik's already asleep.

ELINORE: [*Deflated.*] Oh.

SIMONE: [*Elinore looks so pitiful that Simone sighs, reaches out, and pulls her into the apartment.*] You're here, you might as well come in.

MARVA: Why?

SIMONE: Marva this is my home.

MARVA: And Malik is my grandson!

SIMONE: She just wants to see him, Marva. Surely you can grant her that. [*Marva stifles her outrage and turns away. Simone turns to Elinore.*] You can't wake him.

ELINORE: No, no—I wouldn't dream of it. [*Simone gestures for Elinore to follow her, and the two women exit, leaving Marva and Irene alone. Marva begins pacing, clearly upset. Irene closes the front door and wanders over to the window looking out on the fire escape.*]

MARVA: I swear, I never seen a family of women with more nerve!

IRENE: [*Turns away from the window.*] You've met the daughter?

MARVA: [*Grudgingly.*] No...but I've seen enough of her to know what she's like—bossy, pushy—thinks she owns the world and everyone in it! [*Irene laughs mirthlessly.*] What's so funny?

IRENE: [*Sinks onto the sofa.*] Nothing, really. I think my daughter would describe me in the exact same way.

MARVA: You look like two peas in a pod. I would've guessed you were close.

IRENE: Simone has always preferred her father. She just tolerates me.

MARVA: Well, don't take it personal. She's about to find out just how hard it is to be a good mother.

IRENE: Malik?

MARVA: [*Nods proudly.*] Today the judge granted her sole custody.

49

IRENE: [*Irene shakes her head in disbelief.*] Simone always insisted she didn't want kids.

MARVA: She was just scared, I think.

IRENE: [*Humbled that Marva seems to know something she doesn't.*] Of what?

MARVA: Failure. Simone's a writer—she can put words down on a page and then rearrange them 'til everything's just right. You can't do that with kids. Sometimes you don't get a second chance.

IRENE: So she has control issues. [*Petulant.*] No doubt she blames me for that.

MARVA: Well, like I said. She might appreciate you more once she's walked a mile in your shoes.

IRENE: Simone wants to be nothing like me. Every decision she's made in her life has been a way of defying me. Her sense of style, her career, even her mar—

MARVA: Her marriage? My son wasn't good enough for you either?

IRENE: Connor was a nice young man. He just—I wanted Simone to marry someone who would anchor her, provide her with the security she needs. I mean, she's a—competent writer, and she's had some success with her books, but there's been many a month when Simone simply couldn't make ends meet. She thinks I don't know, but she had to go to her father for help and Charles could never refuse her…Plus she's impulsive. She fired her agent—did she tell you that?

MARVA: [*Clearly troubled by Irene's words.*] No. But maybe she's got another agent lined up—a better one!

IRENE: I wouldn't be surprised. Though I'm sure I'll be the last to know. [*Grows more agitated; turns and looks towards Malik's bedroom.*] What are they doing in there?

MARVA: They'll be out in a minute. Your daughter's got a good heart, I know that much. I'm a Christian woman but there ain't no way I'd a let that woman into my home—to see my child!

IRENE: You blame *her* for Connor's death?

MARVA: 'Course, I do! She put the noose 'round his neck when she gave him away all those years ago.

IRENE: How is what *she* did any different from what *you* did?

MARVA: [*Stunned.*] I gave my boy away so he could have a better life!

IRENE: [*Coolly.*] So did she.

MARVA: I couldn't raise him on my own—I was a single mother!

IRENE: So was she.

MARVA: [*Jumps up and points at Irene, who remains infuriatingly composed.*] You! You're worse than they are—coming into my son's home, ordering folks around like you're some kind of queen! Simone don't even want you here—she'd have thrown you out if that white bitch hadn't shown up!

IRENE: What an interesting *Christian* you are, Marva.

MARVA: Don't you act all high and mighty with me, Miss Thing! I never could understand why a nice girl like Simone didn't want no kids. But now I know! Poor thing probably don't even know what a real mother is. [*Irene reacts.*] You said so yourself—your own daughter can't stand you!

IRENE: [*Finally drawn to her feet, ready to engage.*] Who are you to judge me? Or my daughter! You've got a lot of nerve calling Connor *your son*—you'd only been in his life for a couple of months before he decided to hang himself. I've known you for less than an hour, and that fire escape is starting to look good to ME!

MARVA: I didn't kill Connor—it was your daughter who killed my boy! She wasn't going to marry him—she gave back his ring! She broke his heart doing just what *you* wanted her to do!

IRENE: I think we've established that Simone doesn't follow my advice. If she rejected Connor it could only be because she realized he was unstable…

MARVA: [*Explosive.*] My boy was a saint!

SIMONE: [*Rushes onstage, Elinore trailing behind her.*] What the hell's going on out here? [*There is a pause, and then Marva and Irene simultaneously begin gesturing and blaming one another.*]

MARVA: She said *I* killed Connor!

IRENE: She said *you* did!

SIMONE: [*The back and forth continues until Simone reaches her breaking point.*] ENOUGH! That's it! I've had it—with both of you!

[*From offstage, we hear the sound of a child crying.*] Oh, God—now look what you've done! [*Angry and slightly panicked, Simone rushes offstage to check on Malik. She leaves behind Irene, Marva, and Elinore, who is clearly intimidated and uncomfortable. The women eye one another, but say nothing for a moment.*]

MARVA: Satisfied?

ELINORE: Malik's a beautiful child. Both of you must be very proud. [*Irene and Marva glare at one another but are slightly mollified.*] He looks so much like Connor did at that age…

MARVA: [*Sarcastic.*] You remember?

ELINORE: [*Offended, but afraid to show it.*] Of course, I remember. I've thought of Connor every day since…that time.

MARVA: Hmph. Well, you know what they say—"Outta sight, outta mind."

IRENE: You did a fine job blocking your child out of your mind. But then, I believe you had help…[*She turns to Elinore before Marva can respond.*] I always did wonder how Connor got his name.

ELINORE: [*Delighted to have been addressed.*] Oh! Well, you see—

MARVA: [*Mumbling, but loud enough to be heard.*] No kind of name for a black boy…

IRENE: [*To Marva.*] What did you expect—that they'd call him Tyrone?

ELINORE: [*Finally asserts herself.*] Actually, "Connor" was my husband's choice. It was his mother's maiden name.

IRENE: Irish?

ELINORE: [*Falters, uncertain.*] Uh—Scottish, I think. [*Irene and Marva seem to lose interest in Elinore. She is waiting for Simone to return, but moves towards the door anyway.*] Well…I guess I should go now.

MARVA: I guess so. You got what you came for.

ELINORE: Actually…[*Both Irene and Marva glare at her, daring her to ask for something more.*] Simone said I could have a picture of Malik.

MARVA:  What you need that for?  You just said you got a photographic memory.

SIMONE: [*Enters the room—carrying a drowsy Malik.*]  She's never going to see him again, Marva.  Can you find it within your Christian heart to let her have one photograph?

MARVA: [*Pause.*]  Fine.  [*Grumbles, but snatches up her purse and fishes a photo out of her wallet. She makes an attempt at Christian charity.*]  Here.

ELINORE: [*Accepts the photo and smiles at it for a moment.*]  Thank you.  [*The child's presence seems to have subdued all four women. They look lovingly at him, then away from one another.*]  It's late.  I should go.

IRENE: [*Reaches for her purse, which is on the sofa, and prepares to go.*]  We all should.  [*Marva opens her mouth to object, then glances at Simone and realizes her welcome has finally been worn out.*]

MARVA:  If you need anything—anything at all…

SIMONE:  Thanks, Marva.  I'll call you tomorrow.  Right now, I think both of us just need to get a good night's rest.

MARVA: [*Approaches Simone and caresses Malik.*]  You take care of my baby boy, you hear?  [*Simone smiles and nods wordlessly.*]

IRENE:  You take care of yourself, too.  [*She reaches out and squeezes Simone's arm. Elinore opens the door, and is the first to step out into the hallway. Irene follows her, and finally Marva as well. All three women turn, and look wistfully at the child in Simone's arms.*]

SIMONE: [*Quietly, with forgiveness.*]  Goodnight.  [*She closes the door gently, without waiting for their reply. Malik whimpers and Simone soothes him as she moves over to the sofa and gently eases herself down. She sits for a moment and rocks Malik, inhaling the scent of his skin.*]  You know something, beautiful boy?  You smell just like your daddy…

[*Lights dim, and the backdrop reverts to the opening scene—a dark forest, with random silver birch trees and sheer, brilliantly colored birds weaving through the trees. The same music from the intro begins to play. The silhouette of a man stands near the edge of the "forest." For several moments he watches Simone rocking Malik, then he turns and disappears.*]

## **THE END**

# MOTHER LOAD

A Two-Act Play

by

Zetta Elliott

Copyright © 2007 Zetta Elliott

# MOTHER LOAD

## SYNOPSIS:

A black woman filmmaker in her mid-thirties, Liv, decides to attend her estranged mother's sixtieth birthday party. Her mother, Cleo, is a prolific, celebrated playwright. The event, held over a summer weekend at her mother's New England cottage, has been planned by Freda, Cleo's current lover. The party draws an interesting assortment of guests: Cleo's first female lover, Skye, a white woman poet with whom Cleo had a long-term relationship; Skye's biological daughter, Amy, and her nursing infant; Frank, Cleo's ex-husband; and several other radical feminists of color who have gathered to celebrate Cleo's life. Liv arrives determined to triumphantly disclose her pregnancy, but instead she must confront the fact that Cleo is dying of uterine cancer.

## List of Characters:

**Cleo:** black woman playwright about to turn 60; she is gregarious, magnetic, acerbic, politically engaged; she has won every imaginable award for her plays; mother of Liv; diagnosed with stage-3 uterine cancer

**Olivia:** black woman filmmaker in her mid-thirties; estranged from her mother, she has come to the party in order to gloat over the success of her first film, which was a modest success, and to tell her mother that she is pregnant

**Skye:** a white woman poet in her early 60s; former lover of Cleo; mother of Amy; her poetry has enjoyed only modest success, with her renown diminishing since her break-up with Cleo twelve years ago

| | |
|---|---|
| **Amy**: | a white woman in her mid-thirties; "sister" of Liv, since the two girls grew up together while Skye and Cleo were lovers; now a content, married, stay-at-home mother of three |
| **Freda**: | a Caribbean woman painter in her late 40s; Cleo's current lover |
| **Frank**: | a black man in his late 60s; ex-husband of Cleo and father of Olivia; a successful attorney |
| **Jesse**: | a man (any race) in his late 20s; partner of Liv and father of her unborn child, a cinematographer |

## Setting

A country cottage.

## Time

Summer, now.

## ACT I

### Scene 1

[*Jesse and Olivia enter, struggling with her luggage. Olivia carries her film equipment, while Jesse tries to pull her suitcase over the rugged terrain. They are headed toward Cleo's summer house, which is rustic, and sits on acres of undeveloped land. Jesse and Olivia are clearly urbanites, though Olivia has spent her childhood summers at this house and so is less winded by the journey.*]

OLIVIA: [*Sets her film gear on the porch and goes back to Jesse to retrieve her suitcase.*] Thanks, babe.

JESSE: [*Panting, he hands her the suitcase.*] Tell me again why the road ended a mile back?

OLIVIA: Cleo values her privacy. No road, no visitors.

JESSE: [*Stops and looks at the rather modest cottage.*] So. This is where the great Cleo Banks writes her Pulitzer prize-winning plays?

OLIVIA: [*Fishes in her bag for a bottle of water.*] You're not going to start gushing again, are you? [*She opens the bottle, takes a sip, and hands it to Jesse.*]

JESSE: [*Accepts the bottle and sucks at it thirstily.*] Does this place even have running water?

OLIVIA: It didn't when we first moved in. There used to be an outhouse out back, and one of those hand crank pumps. Skye made Mom fix the place up. I spent nearly all my summers here. [*She shrugs, dismissing the memory.*] But Cleo's gone soft in her old age—now there's a hot tub, a dishwasher. She's probably even got a satellite dish hidden around here somewhere.

JESSE: [*He looks up towards the roof.*] Are those solar panels?

OLIVIA: Mm hm. This place has its own water supply, its own generator. There's a huge organic garden over there. The only mother Cleo respects is Mother Earth.

JESSE: I thought you'd be roughing it this weekend. Looks like you'll be living in the lap of luxury.

OLIVIA: Hardly. It'll be a lesbian love-fest—a bunch of crazy old dykes prancing around without bras, singing protest songs from the '70s.

JESSE: You did bring a gift, right? It's not every day your brilliant mother turns sixty.

OLIVIA: I didn't come here to kiss up, Jesse.

JESSE: I know. But a little grease might help the wheels turn more smoothly…

OLIVIA: Don't, ok?

JESSE: You know I'd never ask you to compromise your artistic integrity. [*Liv looks unimpressed.*] She's your mother, Liv. Did it ever occur to you she might actually *want* to help us out?

OLIVIA: Trust me—we can't afford Cleo's "help." I'd rather die than ask her for money.

JESSE: You're not asking for a handout—it would be an investment. If you're not comfortable making a business proposition, then let me try pitching the film…

OLIVIA: [*Snorts derisively.*] Are you wearing a cup?

JESSE: I'm not afraid of your mother, Liv.

OLIVIA: You should be.

JESSE: Can't I at least stay for lunch?

OLIVIA: We talked about this already, hon.

JESSE: I know. But this is a family event—and I'm family now, right?

OLIVIA: Baby steps, remember? Cleo doesn't even know we're married.

JESSE: So we'll tell her—together. And then we can tell her about—

OLIVIA: [*Kisses him to preempt the conversation.*] I'll call if I need you to come rescue me.

JESSE: Your mother's not a monster, Liv.

OLIVIA: One day you'll understand.

JESSE: One day, say, nine months from now? [*She frowns and so he kisses her again.*] I'm kidding. You know you're going to be an amazing mother.

OLIVIA: [*Steps back to make the parting final.*] I'll call you. [*Jesse nods and withdraws. Olivia watches him go, then turns and looks at the cottage. Taking a deep breath, she picks up her bag and goes up on the porch. She doesn't hear Skye approach.*]

SKYE: Liv?

OLIVIA: [*Turns and sees her former stepmother.*] Skye? [*Delighted, she drops her things and runs back down the porch, throwing herself into Skye's open arms. The two women hold one another for a long moment, rocking slightly.*]

SKYE: [*Pulls back and touches Liv's face with maternal tenderness.*] I'm so glad you're here.

OLIVIA: You're the one I really wanted to see. I've missed you. [*They embrace once more, then move to the porch and sit down on the steps.*]

SKYE: You look good, Liv. [*Playful, confidential.*] Married life must agree with you!

OLIVIA: [*Blushes and laughs.*] You just missed Jesse—he wanted to stay, but…he doesn't really understand what he's gotten himself into.

SKYE: He's into *you*—that's all that matters. We are going to meet him someday, aren't we?

OLIVIA: Sure! I just…I didn't know what—how she would be this weekend. We haven't spoken in more than a year.

SKYE: I know. I'm really glad you came, Liv. It'll mean a lot to Cleo.

OLIVIA: Is the gang all here?

SKYE: Almost. We were up pretty late last night—most of them are still sleeping it off.

OLIVIA: You all are some tough old broads.

SKYE: [*Laughs.*] Well, I tell you, I was feeling my age this morning…but it's good to be back. Amy should be here later this afternoon.

OLIVIA: She's coming?

SKYE: Of course! She wouldn't miss your mother's birthday party—and a chance to see you again.

OLIVIA: I just—I guess I figured she was too busy. I mean, it can't be easy traveling with three kids.

SKYE: Well, she's only bringing the youngest one—Carter isn't weaned yet, so he needs to be close to his mom.

OLIVIA: God, three kids.

SKYE: I know! I never really thought of myself as a grandma, but it's actually not that bad. Amy brings them over for an afternoon, and then she takes them home a few hours later. It's great, really—all the fun and just a fraction of the work! I'd highly recommend grandmotherhood.

OLIVIA: Are you still writing?

SKYE: Mm hm. Cleo put me in the cabin by the lake. It's perfect for writing—quiet, secluded. Of course, all that will change once Amy arrives with Carter! But I think I'm going to stay for a couple of weeks. I want to spend some time with your mother.

OLIVIA: What about Freda?

SKYE: What about her?

OLIVIA: Isn't it—I don't know—awkward having her around?

SKYE: She's a wonderful woman, Liv—and an outstanding artist. You should take a look at her studio while you're here. There's a portrait of Cleo I've got my eye on…

OLIVIA: And it doesn't bother you that she's…taken your place?

SKYE: Your mother and I separated twelve years ago, Liv. Freda isn't the first lover your mother has taken. But she won't ever take my place. No one will.

OLIVIA: Isn't it funny how Amy and I grew up in this…"alternate environment," yet now we're both married, we're both—[*Stops short of admitting her pregnancy.*]

SKYE: Normal? Sane? We were talking about that last night—how radical women seem to raise conservative kids.

OLIVIA: Well, I wouldn't exactly call myself conservative.

SKYE: [*Knowing.*] No, I wouldn't call you that either.

OLIVIA: It's just—there was a lot of….upheaval in my life. I needed to finally settle down, root myself somewhere. With someone stable, someone I could rely on.

SKYE: [*Slightly hurt.*] Cleo and I—we always thought our lifestyle would open up possibilities for you girls. We never meant to scare you back into the box.

OLIVIA: I know—and it wasn't fear that drove us away. Not for me, at least. Cleo was so brave—she was always dancing on the razor's edge. I wanted to be like her, but…I don't know. I guess maybe I was ashamed of how much I needed her—how much I wanted her to need me. She doesn't need anyone, does she?

SKYE: [*Wants to say something, but decides to wait. She strokes Liv's hair.*] "No man's an island."

OLIVIA: [*Tries to be light, but fails.*] Ah, but Cleo Banks is a WOMAN—hear her roar!

SKYE: She's human, Liv. We see our mothers as giants, but they're not invincible.

OLIVIA: Really? Cleo does a damn good impersonation of Superwoman.

SKYE: Would you let her be weak?

OLIVIA: Let her? Since when does Cleo need my permission to do anything? [*Skye again nearly speaks, but instead holds her tongue.*] I used to envy Amy when we were growing up.

SKYE: Why?

OLIVIA: Because Amy was your pearl. To Cleo, I was just an irritant.

SKYE: Your mother loves you, Liv. She always has.

OLIVIA: Only because she made her mind up to do it. Cleo was determined to tolerate me.

SKYE: Don't be so hard on her. Your mother's had an extraordinary life, but don't think she doesn't have regrets.

OLIVIA: Yeah—all the time she wasted trying to control her "wild child."

SKYE: Cleo was always proud of your "wayward tendencies." She never wanted an ordinary child.

OLIVIA: She never wanted a child, period.

SKYE: That's not true. She could have found a way to terminate the pregnancy. It wouldn't have been easy, but we knew enough people back then…

OLIVIA: Frank wouldn't have let her have an abortion.

SKYE: Does Jesse tell you what to do with your body?

OLIVIA: [*Silently concedes the point.*] Cleo thought she wanted to be married. Then she met you, and changed her mind. You can divorce your husband, but what do you do with a kid you no longer want? Cleo cut the cord before I was even born.

SKYE: I'm sorry you see things that way, Liv.

OLIVIA: [*Rises from the steps, and begins pacing, trying to contain her anger.*] Oh, God, Skye—please don't tell me you respect "my truth." It's not *my* truth—it's THE truth! Cleo never wanted me! [*The front door of the cottage opens and Cleo slowly emerges. She squints, despite the shade of the porch, and Freda immediately comes up behind her with a hat, a sweater, and some thick, black sunglasses used by cataract patients.*]

CLEO: Oh, Lord! [*Her voice is hoarse, and she wavers on her feet. She reaches for the shades and dons them while Freda fusses with the hat and sweater. Cleo allows herself to be dressed, but barely acknowledges Freda's assistance. It is a warm summer day, yet Cleo is swathed in layers of clothing. To Skye.*] What time did you get up?

SKYE: [*Turns her body so she can see Cleo.*] Five thirty.

CLEO: Good God—why?

SKYE: After twenty years of rising at dawn, I can't seem to help myself.

[*Cleo moves towards the steps and grasps the railing. She irritably kicks at the bags Olivia has left on the porch. Freda holds her by the waist and arm. Olivia tries to compose herself. She swallows her anger and tries not to show her disdain for her mother's condition. She assumes Cleo is hung over from the night before.*]

CLEO: I want to sit in the sun. [*Skye rises and Freda hands Cleo over before disappearing inside. Skye assists Cleo as she slowly descends the stairs and guides her over to a bench in the front yard. After lowering Cleo onto the bench, Skye sits down beside her and adjusts the sweater.*]

SKYE: Look who's here, Cleo.

CLEO: [*Grunts.*] The prodigal.

OLIVIA: [*Steps forward.*] Hello, Cleo. Happy Birthday.

CLEO: It's tomorrow.

OLIVIA: [*Testily.*] I know.

SKYE: Liv brought her camera. She's offered to tape tomorrow's festivities.

CLEO: Extra footage for your next exposé?

SKYE: Cleo—

CLEO: What? She's a chip off the old block—you got a real flair for the dramatic, kid. But you should have cast Angela Bassett in my role. That B-movie actress you used—she was a little heavy-handed, I thought. But then, maybe you directed her to act over the top…

OLIVIA: Well, you are larger than life, Cleo. [*Bitter.*] I didn't have the budget to hire big name stars.

CLEO: I guess you can't really expect much from an indie.

SKYE: I thought your film was wonderful, Liv. And you got some really good reviews.

OLIVIA: The *Times* said it showed promise. [*Pointedly, to Cleo.*] There's more to come.

SKYE: [*Worried.*] Really? Are you working on another film already?

CLEO: It's a sequel to Mommy Dearest: *The Bitch is Back.*

OLIVIA: [*Ignores Cleo and speaks to Skye.*] We're still getting our funding together, but yes—I've finished another script.

CLEO: Something original, I hope. If you keep writing about your evil, heartless mother, and your terrible, tear-filled childhood, folks will think you're just a one-trick pony.

OLIVIA: You only write plays.

CLEO: Form and content, my dear. They're two entirely different things.

OLIVIA: [*Sarcastic.*] Thanks for the tip.

CLEO: You could use a few pointers.

OLIVIA: [*Bristles, but acts open.*] Such as?

CLEO: Characters should be authentic creations with distinct voices—not thinly-veiled caricatures who serve as mouthpieces for your own personal angst.

SKYE: Cleo—

OLIVIA: No, no, Skye—let her continue. It's not every day that I get free advice from my accomplished mother.

CLEO: Hmph. My opinion is the one thing about me you *don't* value.

OLIVIA: Meaning?

CLEO: Meaning you wouldn't have a career if it weren't for me. You're simply trading off *my* hard-earned reputation—*my* achievements—*my* name.

OLIVIA: God—your arrogance is unreal! Is it so hard for you to believe that people might actually be interested in ME? In m*y* stories, *my* vision of the world? I do have my own voice, Cleo.

CLEO: [*Sighs as though bored.*] But what do you have to say? Eventually people will get tired of your whining and complaining, Liv. You're hardly a poster child for misery and misfortune. [*Suddenly vicious.*] You had every advantage—every opportunity!

OLIVIA: I'm just an ungrateful wretch, aren't I, Cleo? And you—you're a saint better yet, a martyr! The struggling artist who made every sacrifice for her darling child. Is that the film you want me to make?

CLEO: Why not? It couldn't be any worse than that other load of crap you pulled out your—

FREDA: Tea! [*Freda reemerges from the house, carrying a tray. She carefully steps over the bags on the porch, then descends the steps and sets the tray on a table next to Skye. Olivia, furious, tries to walk it off. Skye begins preparing a cup of tea for Cleo, while Freda goes back up the steps to gather Olivia's bags.*]

OLIVIA: Here, I'll do that.

FREDA: I don't know where to put you.

OLIVIA: Put me? What are you talking about? I'll just stay in my old room.

FREDA: [*Glances at Skye and Cleo.*] Other guests are already settled in the spare room. I didn't realize you were coming...

OLIVIA: [*Angry.*] I emailed you weeks ago—I told you I was coming.

FREDA: I know, but your mother said—I suppose we could make room, if you don't mind sleeping on the couch...

OLIVIA: [*Outraged.*] The couch!

SKYE: [*Hands Cleo her tea cup and comes over to the porch.*] Why don't you and Amy stay out in the cabin, Liv? I'll move my things back in here. It makes more sense, really—you girls won't want to be up all night, listening to us reminisce. [*She takes up one of Liv's bags and tries to guide her into the house.*] That'll work, right?

OLIVIA: [*Shoots a deadly glance at her mother and grabs the rest of her bags from Freda.*] Whatever. [*Olivia stomps inside the house. Skye and Freda share a worried glance, then both look over at Cleo. She is seated contentedly on the bench, sipping her tea and enjoying the bright sunshine. Skye and Freda enter the house.*]

## ACT I

## Scene 2

[*Olivia and Amy enter the tiny cabin out by the lake. We hear the sounds of crickets, and as the door opens, distant laughter from the other women at the cottage. Olivia holds the door open as Amy enters, carrying her sleeping child in a portable car seat. Amy seems very at ease, but Olivia is nervous, anxious to do all she can to assist with the child. The cabin itself is cozy but far from luxurious; it is furnished with old, mismatched furniture, though hand-made curtains and a quilt on the double bed make the cabin homey. There is a tiny bathroom in one corner, with towels hung on a rack on the door. There is a chest of drawers and a small desk with a vase holding wildflowers.*]

AMY: I hope I have that kind of stamina when I'm sixty. They're so—alive!

OLIVIA: They're drunk, Amy—and stoned out of their minds! Apparently, Cleo's still tending to her little "herb garden."

AMY: [*Laughs and sets the baby carrier down in a corner. She peers at the sleeping child and then falls back on the bed.*] I'm beat.

OLIVIA: You really didn't have to come, you know. You could have just called or sent a card. Cleo would have understood.

AMY: [*Props herself up on her elbow so she can see Liv.*] I know. But I wanted to see you. It's been ages, you know. The last time I saw you was at your college graduation.

OLIVIA: [*Somewhat abashed.*] Yeah—I'm sorry about missing your wedding, Amy. I really wanted to be there, but—I was on the road with this production team, and we were shooting this documentary in India, and my girlfriend—well, she was my boss at first, and then we kind of got involved…but then we broke up and it was really awful, having to work with her every day—she would have fired me if I just walked off the set…

AMY: You lead such an exciting life, Liv! I always thought I'd travel, live abroad, have endless affairs. [*She laughs and falls back on the bed.*] And now look at me.

OLIVIA: [*Wanders over to the baby and peers down at him.*] You're amazing, Amy. I don't know how you do it.

AMY: Do what?

OLIVIA: Motherhood, marriage. How do you make it work?

AMY: Well, I had to accept that it *is* work. That's the hardest part, really. Having this dream, and then waking up day after day and finally realizing that it's never going to be perfect. [*She yawns.*] I'm tired all the time.

OLIVIA: But you don't regret it.

AMY: [*Becomes thoughtful.*] No. I wouldn't trade my children for anything. But it's hard work, Liv. And unbelievably expensive.

OLIVIA: Ben makes good money, doesn't he?

AMY: Not enough for us to put the kids in daycare. That was the plan initially. We'd have one kid, I'd stay home for a year, then we'd put the kid in daycare and I'd go back to work.

OLIVIA: So what happened?

AMY: [*She laughs.*] Kid #2 happened! I couldn't go back to work when I knew I'd be out on maternity leave again in just a few months. And now I have Carter…once the kids are all in school, maybe then I'll go back to work.

OLIVIA: Maybe you should just take a break. Do you still dance?

AMY: Not really. My body's shot to hell, and I don't have the time or the energy to practice every day.

OLIVIA: Dance was your passion. You even managed to teach my two left feet a few moves. Remember that little routine we used to do?

[*Liv fumbles through a few moves until Amy drags herself up and takes Liv through the routine. They are playful, young, silly. When the dance is complete, Amy drops onto the bed once more.*]

AMY: I was a different person back then. I've got other priorities now. [*There is a pause; Amy rolls over so she can look at Liv.*] Why did you decide to get married, Liv?

OLIVIA: [*Shrugs, and sinks into one of the mismatched chairs.*] I guess I was ready.

AMY: Don't take this the wrong way, but I always thought you preferred women. Are you bisexual now?

OLIVIA: I don't know—I don't really call myself anything anymore. Jesse and I are on the same path, that's all. We're committed to the same things. We're compatible.

AMY: Why didn't you tell Cleo?

OLIVIA: [*Groans.*] Because I wanted to *enjoy* the experience—without any drama, without all the judgment she brings to everything. Jesse's nearly ten years younger than me, and you know how Cleo feels about men.

AMY: My mom gets along with Ben.

OLIVIA: Your mom's normal, Amy. [*Amy challenges her with a glance.*] Relatively speaking. Skye told me she loves being a grandma.

AMY: Sure—for a few hours at a time. For a while, Ben and I talked about moving so we could be closer to her. But when I mentioned it to Mom, she freaked out! You and I grew up with two mothers and a whole slew of aunts in the house, yet Mom expects me to raise these kids on my own. So much for "it takes a village."

OLIVIA: What did you expect, Amy? Skye's still a poet. Why do you think she and Cleo kept all those "aunts" around? So they could hand us off to them and go work on their latest masterpiece.

AMY: [*Sighs.*] I know. I just thought…I don't know. I thought it would be different after all these years. I didn't think her writing would still come first. I mean, when I was dancing—even when dance was *my life*—I still knew I wanted kids. I always believed there'd be room for a family.

OLIVIA: There's room because you *made* room. That's what real power does—it lets you decide how you want things to be. [*Pause.*] Can I tell you something?

AMY: Sure.

OLIVIA: I'm pregnant.

AMY: [*Laughs.*] I know.

OLIVIA: You know? How? [*She jumps up and searches the room for a mirror.*] I'm not showing yet—am I?

AMY: You have what is commonly referred to as "the glow"—which is the first indication that your body is no longer your own.

OLIVIA: [*Finds a small face mirror and stands before it, transfixed.*] I'm glowing?

AMY: It's not like a halo or anything. You just—you sit differently in your skin. You're a host now. It's a different way of being in your body.

OLIVIA: Shit. [*Turns away from the mirror to face Amy.*] Does anyone else know?

AMY: I doubt it. Like you said, the old gals are hammered. Why—are you going to keep that a secret, too?

OLIVIA: No. It's why I came here, really. I want Cleo to know. I need her to know she didn't crush the maternal instinct in me.

AMY: Damn, Liv.

OLIVIA: You don't know what it's like, Amy. Skye adored you.

AMY: In the past, maybe. But I think she always wished I'd been more like you—more adventurous. She'd never admit it, but I know I disappointed my mother.

OLIVIA: Get out of here.

AMY: I'm serious, Liv. My relationship with Skye has never been as…contentious as your relationship with Cleo, but that doesn't mean it's perfect. Look at me—look at what I've become: a suburban housewife with three kids. I didn't even marry anyone interesting or "exotic"—Ben's about as WASPy as you can get. I can't imagine what Skye tells her friends when they sit around and compare notes.

OLIVIA: You really think they do that?

AMY: I bet they're doing it right now. We're talking about them.

OLIVIA: [*Pause.*] Well, your mom did say they'd been talking about us last night. They were wondering why militant left-wing mothers raise conservative daughters.

AMY: I guess radical lesbian feminists can't count on their DNA.

OLIVIA: Or their example.

AMY: Sometimes I wonder if I married Ben just so I could have a man in my life. I never knew my dad. My life was always filled with women.

OLIVIA: Not just any women—strong, powerful, AMAZON women!

AMY: Warrior women! [*They fall out, laughing, and the baby awakes with a feeble cry.*] He's probably hungry. [*Amy gets up off the bed and lifts her son from his carrier. She sits on the edge of the bed and discreetly lifts her top to feed him. Olivia watches, slightly uncomfortable but unable to look away.*]

OLIVIA: What's it feel like?

AMY: [*Glances up at Liv, then looks adoringly at her son.*] It kind of hurts at first. It's the strangest sensation—not exactly pleasure, but—it's incredibly satisfying. Feeding my kids makes me feel…important.

OLIVIA: [*Draws closer, almost against her will. She gently perches on the edge of the bed.*] I used to think women who breastfed were like animals. I called them cows.

AMY: When my daughter was born, I had too much milk. No matter how much I expressed, my breasts were always full and sore—I was soaking through all my shirts. I didn't want to, but I finally broke down and borrowed a friend's electric pump. Sitting there, strapped into that thing—I felt like an animal. [*They sit silently for a moment, watching the infant feed.*]

OLIVIA: Why didn't they want this for us?

AMY: I guess…they wanted us to be…free. Not tethered or bound to anything.

OLIVIA: Cleo always made me feel like children were a curse. She said motherhood was like death to a woman artist.

AMY:  Children *are* work, Liv—don't kid yourself about that.  Have you thought about how you'll balance making films and being a mom?

OLIVIA:  I'll have Jesse to help me, and—well—we'll just try to make it work.

AMY:  And if it doesn't?

OLIVIA:  [*Rises and paces the room.*]  If it doesn't work—if I can't do both—then I'll choose.  I'll choose my kid, and I won't blame her for ruining my life.

AMY:  Is that why you want this baby?  So you can prove you're a better mother than Cleo?

OLIVIA:  I'm not trying to prove anything.

AMY:  [*Rises and places the baby back in his carrier.  She moves over to her bags and begins preparing for bed.*]  You know, Liv, your mom isn't doing so well.

OLIVIA:  What are you talking about?  Cleo's having a ball up there.

AMY:  My mother asked me not to tell you this, but—

OLIVIA:  Tell me what?

AMY:  Cleo's sick, Liv.

OLIVIA:  Sick—with what?

AMY:  I don't know all the details, but—

OLIVIA:  But what?

AMY:  If there are things you want to say to her…you should say them now.  Don't wait.

OLIVIA:  [*Incredulous, sarcastic.*]  You're saying she's dying?

AMY:  I don't know, Liv, I really don't.  But you see how she looks.

OLIVIA:  She looks fine!  She's lost a few pounds, but she had a few to spare.  Cleo's the same as ever—she's the life of the party!

AMY:  Maybe you don't notice because you haven't seen her in a while…

OLIVIA:  Oh—is that what this is?  Now Cleo's the victim and I'm the big, bad daughter?

AMY: [*Glances at her sleeping child.*] Jesus, Liv—calm down. I'm not accusing you of anything. I'm just saying…things have happened since you left.

OLIVIA: If Cleo's sick, why didn't anyone tell me?

AMY: Mom says Freda's been managing your mother's care.

OLIVIA: I don't like that woman. She put her cronies in our old room. We should be sleeping in the big house, not out here in the quarters!

AMY: Freda's—well, I guess she's like an herbalist.

OLIVIA: She sure was sucking on that "herb" tonight.

AMY: No, I mean she's into holistic healing—non-traditional medicine.

OLIVIA: She could be a voodoo priestess for all I care. What's it got to do with my mom?

AMY: Well, Skye thinks Freda convinced your mother to stop seeing her doctor.

OLIVIA: [*Pause.*] And?

AMY: And…Cleo doesn't seem to be getting better. In fact, Skye thinks she's getting worse. [*Olivia moves over to the cabin's one window and pulls back the curtain. She squints at the "big house," trying to discern remote faces and voices. Faint raucous laughter filters down to the lake. Amy moves over to the bathroom and takes a towel off the rack.*] I'm not trying to freak you out, Liv. I know you came here to…accomplish certain things. But Cleo's not up for a fight right now.

OLIVIA: [*Continues staring out the window.*] Oh yeah? You should have heard her this afternoon. Cleo's tongue is still in good working order.

AMY: Just—go easy on her, Liv. Okay? [*Pause.*] Liv?

OLIVIA: [*Without turning, nods slightly to acknowledge Amy.*] I hear you.

AMY: [*Glances at her son once more.*] I'm going to take a quick shower. Can you keep an eye on Carter?

OLIVIA: [*Finally pulls herself away from the window.*] Sure, go ahead.

AMY: Thanks. [*Amy enters the bathroom and closes the door; the shower starts a moment later. Olivia crosses the tiny room and sits in a chair next to the baby carrier. She somberly observes the sleeping infant.*]

## ACT I

## Scene 3

[*The garden outside of Cleo's cottage. It is a bright, sunny morning. Freda is hard at work, pulling weeds, hoeing, gathering ripe vegetables, etc. Her head is wrapped with a kerchief. Skye is there as well, wearing a floppy sun hat. She is quietly admiring the flowers, occasionally pruning a bloom and adding it to her basket. Liv approaches, wet from her recent swim in the lake. Skye greets her with genuine warmth; Freda ignores Liv and continues working vigorously as though to prove a point.*]

SKYE: Good morning! How's the water?

OLIVIA: Cold. Amy's still down there with Carter.

SKYE: I might join them in a minute. It's hot as hell out here. [*She fans herself and gazes at Liv, pleased.*] The sun's kinder to you—you're glowing. [*Freda glances at Liv and Liv blushes, suddenly self-conscious.*]

OLIVIA: Yeah, I—I should probably put on some sunscreen or something.

SKYE: You don't burn, do you? We never put anything on you girls when you were young. You used to run around naked from sun up to sun down—by the end of the summer, you were the color of cinnamon, and Amy was like unbuttered toast—just a bit crisp. [*Laughs gaily.*] I'm making myself hungry—have you eaten yet?

OLIVIA: No, I was just going to forage for something now.

FREDA: [*Abruptly stops what she is doing and heads for the back door. Brusque.*] How you like your eggs?

OLIVIA: I can get my own breakfast—I'm sure I remember where everything is.

FREDA: The kitchen's been rearranged. It's best if you just tell me what you want.

OLIVIA: You know what, Freda? This is *my* home. [*Skye, sensing the tension between them, tries to intervene.*]

SKYE: Liv, why don't we make Amy a frittata—remember how she used to love eating fresh tomatoes from the garden? Freda, could we steal one of your...

FREDA: [*Hefts the bushel basket of vegetables onto the back porch and resumes her work.*] Help yourself.

[*Skye glances at Liv before picking the choicest vegetables from the basket. Liv watches Freda with obvious contempt, then heads past Skye for the door.*]

SKYE: Liv?

OLIVIA: I need to see my mother.

FREDA: [*Stands abruptly.*] Cleo's sleeping—you can't disturb her.

OLIVIA: [*Spins, wanting the confrontation.*] Who the fuck are you to tell me what I can and cannot do?

SKYE: Liv...

FREDA: [*Calm, yet defiant.*] Cleo needs to rest now. She cannot tolerate any—aggravation.

OLIVIA: Aggravation!

FREDA: Agitation, then. Whatever it is you want to say, it will have to wait.

OLIVIA: Bitch, you must be out your mind if you think I'm going to stand here and let you pencil me in. I'm her *daughter*. You're nothing more than the flavor of the week. You cook, you clean, you sweep up the yard—that makes you the hired help—*not* Miss Anne.

SKYE: Liv, please. Don't do this—not today.

OLIVIA: Stay out of this, Skye. You should have told me yesterday—you should have told me as soon as you knew!

SKYE: Knew what, Liv?

OLIVIA: That Cleo's sick. What's wrong with her? Never mind, get out of my way. [*Liv attempts to push past Skye, who reaches out to restrain her. As Liv fights to free herself, two other women exit the house and with Freda, form a blockade before the back door. Liv, sensing their determination to thwart her, flings herself back, enraged.*] What the fuck is this? Get out of my way! You can't keep me from her—she's my mother! She's my mother!

SKYE: [*Tries to approach Liv, who is agitated and aggressive.*] Liv—Liv, please, try to calm down.

OLIVIA: Amy told me—I know all about that…witch! [*She points at Freda, who remains impassive.*] I'm taking my mother to a doctor. I'm taking her away from here!

FREDA: Cleo's not going anywhere.

OLIVIA: [*To Skye.*] You're letting this happen? You're just going to stand by and let them murder my mother?

SKYE: [*Finally succeeds in getting close enough to Liv to seize her by the arms.*] Liv, please, take a walk with me and I'll tell you everything…

OLIVIA: [*Rips herself away.*] I don't want to take a goddamn walk! I want you to tell me the truth!

SKYE: [*Tries again to get close to Liv.*] Ok, ok. I'll tell you what I know. Ok?

OLIVIA: [*Panting, frantic, glances at the three women on the porch, then looks at Skye.*] What's wrong with Cleo?

SKYE: [*Takes a deep breath and speaks slowly, as if to a child.*] She was diagnosed with uterine cancer more than a year ago. [*Olivia stills, and Skye tries again to touch her; this time Liv doesn't pull back.*]

SKYE: Cleo got a second opinion, and the specialist confirmed the diagnosis. So your mother started chemotherapy and radiation.

FREDA: Them damn doctors nearly killed her, you know. [*The other two women murmur and nod sympathetically.*]

SKYE: [*Turns Liv's face so that she is focusing only on her words.*] The cancer didn't respond to the treatment, and the doctor wanted to operate—

FREDA: [*Sucks her teeth.*] Blood-thirsty thief, dem!

SKYE: But Cleo didn't want a hysterectomy. So she opted for a different course of treatment. Something more…holistic.

OLIVIA: [*To Skye.*] But it's not working, is it? [*To Freda.*] You fucking witch doctor! You're poisoning my mother!

SKYE: [*Grabs hold of Liv again, whose strength seems to be flagging.*] No, no, Liv—it's not like that, it's not like that at all. Liv, honey, your mother…Cleo's very sick.

OLIVIA: [*Starts heaving with sobs that won't break.*] Oh, God…Oh, God…[*From within, Cleo calls for Freda, who responds instantly. The other two women remain "on guard." Liv sinks to her knees, clutching her belly. Skye tries unsuccessfully to soothe her. Frank comes around the side of the house.*]

FRANK: Is anybody home? [*He sees Skye and bursts into a smile.*] Hey, Skye! The front door was locked, so I—[*He sees his daughter on the ground and rushes over.*] Olivia? Baby?

OLIVIA: [*Looks up and throws herself against her father.*] Daddy!

SKYE: [*Sighs heavily and backs away from the pair. To no one in particular.*] I'm going down to the lake. [*Skye exits, wearily. Assured by Liv's state, the two women turn and reenter the house, leaving Liv and Frank alone. He holds his daughter, rocking her gently to soothe her. After a while, she quiets.*]

FRANK: There, that's better. Now tell me what happened.

OLIVIA: [*Sniffs and messily wipes her face against her father's shirt.*] Mom's sick. [*Frank's face stiffens, but he continues to rock Liv.*] I think she may be dying. [*When Frank still does not respond, Liv pulls back and searches his face.*] You knew.

FRANK: I told Cleo she should tell you. I always felt you had a right to know.

OLIVIA: [*Pulls herself further away, petulant.*] What is this? Some kind of special club that everyone gets to join except me?

FRANK: I'm sorry, Olivia. I was trying to respect your mother's wishes.

OLIVIA: She told you not to tell me? What the fuck is that? Cleo excommunicates me and then tries to die behind my back?

FRANK: I think she wanted to protect you—

OLIVIA: Oh, *please*, Dad. Since when did Cleo ever give a damn about *my* safety, or *my* needs?

FRANK: Listen, Liv—I know things haven't been right between you and your mother—

OLIVIA: [*Stands, takes a deep breath. Liv straightens herself out and begins to walk it off, reasoning with herself.*] You know what? I'm good. I can handle this.

FRANK: Liv, you don't have to pretend—

OLIVIA: No, no, Dad—I really am ok with this. You know why? Because this is nothing new. In fact, this is par for the course with Cleo. This is her final masterpiece—her magnum opus. [*She laughs harshly.*] Her swan song, if you will.

FRANK: [*Tries to reach for her.*] Liv—

OLIVIA: [*Steers herself away from him.*] I'll bet she scripted this entire scene. And here I am, playing the grieving daughter, wracked with guilt—playing it to a tee! [*Forces a sharp laugh.*] *Damn*, she's good!

FRANK: [*Stern.*] Olivia, that's enough. This is no laughing matter.

OLIVIA: You're right, Dad—this isn't a comedy at all. It's a tragedy, her finest oeuvre.

FRANK: I'm not enjoying this performance, Liv. You shouldn't mock your mother's condition.

OLIVIA: [*Sobers.*] What do you want me to say, Dad? I won't let this destroy me.

FRANK: This isn't about you.

OLIVIA: [*Somewhat shamed, turns away from him.*] You should have heard her yesterday. I never would have guessed she was nearing the end. Even with her last few breaths, Cleo was cursing me.

FRANK: Don't you think, Liv—that maybe now's the time to raise the white flag.

OLIVIA: [*Quietly.*] Surrender?

FRANK: [*Draws closer to her.*] Don't you want to stop fighting your mother?

OLIVIA: [*Spins around.*] Of course, I do! You think I like being treated this way? You think I want her to hate me?

FRANK: Your mother doesn't hate you, Liv. She loves you.

OLIVIA: [*Shakes her head and starts pacing again.*] Cleo doesn't approve of me—she doesn't respect the choices I've made. Just once….just once I wanted to make her feel proud to be my mother.

FRANK: This could be that moment, Liv.

OLIVIA: I don't know how to please her, Dad. What does she want from me? Should I go to her and fall on my knees? Should I beg for forgiveness? Or would she want me to be strong—no tears, no fear, no flinching before death.

FRANK: She'd want you to be genuine, Liv. You don't have to audition for your mother—you've already got the role.

OLIVIA: [*Against her will, she starts to cry once more.*] It's too soon. I'm not ready to lose her—not yet, not for good.

FRANK: [*Walks over and enfolds his daughter in his arms.*] Neither am I, baby. Neither am I.

OLIVIA: [*Allows herself to be held, consoled by her father. Finally she pushes him away.*] It's different for you. You have another family—another wife. I won't ever have another mother.

FRANK: You have Skye. And now you have Jesse. You know you'll always have me. [*She looks at him, and he sees his own mortality.*] What can I tell you, Liv? None of us will be here forever.

OLIVIA: [*Steps back into her father's embrace.*] I'm glad you came.

FRANK: Me, too.

OLIVIA: I've got news. I wanted to tell you and Cleo together, but…

FRANK: What is it, hon?

OLIVIA: [*Bashful.*] I'm pregnant.

FRANK: [*Thrilled.*] Ha ha! [*He grabs Liv and gives her a squeeze.*] That's my girl! Is it a boy?

OLIVIA: [*Playfully slaps at him.*] It's too soon to tell. You don't want another girl?

FRANK: I want a healthy grandchild. But after four daughters, a boy would mix things up a little. And I'd finally have an ally…

OLIVIA: I'm still on your side!

FRANK: You're the only one.

OLIVIA: That's not true. Wanda always backs you up.

FRANK: I know. But when she and the girls get together—when they shop, or cook, or—whatever they do...I'm not a part of it. It's the same way I feel when I come up here. Like I'm very...unnecessary. I've missed you, Liv. It's different when you're around.

OLIVIA: Because I'm not a girly-girl? Because I can talk politics—and sports?

FRANK: Because you have...depth, complexity. You're an interesting person, Liv. Your view of the world is absolutely unique. You're like your mother in that way. We had a lot of trouble in our marriage, but with Cleo, I was never bored. We always had great...conversation.

OLIVIA: It couldn't have been easy, living with a genius.

FRANK: Well, Cleo didn't become a genius until after she left me for Skye.

OLIVIA: [*Tries to recall the order of things.*] After I was born?

FRANK: [*Nods.*] She was already writing when we met, but Cleo finished her first really great play about a year after you were born. *Mississippi Rhapsody.* It won an Obie.

OLIVIA: You don't think I—held her back?

FRANK: Of course, you didn't! If anything, you made Cleo that much more determined to succeed. Suddenly she was...focused, driven.

OLIVIA: [*Bitter.*] Desperate.

FRANK: Cleo wasn't cut out for the suburbs, Liv. She may not have been June Cleaver, but you can't deny that you've been the beneficiary of her success. You went to private schools, an ivy league college, then the top film school. You've traveled all over the world. I couldn't have given you that on my own.

OLIVIA: I never asked for a silver spoon.

FRANK: [*Gently.*] Still, "to whom much is given..."

OLIVIA: I don't know what she expects of me. Skye says Cleo admires my independence, yet she won't tolerate any kind of defiance. I can't be her puppet.

FRANK: You can be yourself without being—

OLIVIA: [*Defensive.*] What?

FRANK: Vindictive. Your film hurt her, Liv.

OLIVIA: I didn't mean for it to be taken literally.

FRANK: Didn't you? Your mother's a public figure. You had to know the press would smell blood in the water.

OLIVIA: So what—it's my job to protect her? Now I'm the parent?

FRANK: You're no longer a child, Liv.

OLIVIA: Like I said, my film was an interpretation of my childhood. It's not like I made the whole thing up.

FRANK: You could have, you know.

OLIVIA: What?

FRANK: You're an artist, Liv. Use your imagination. [*Pause.*] Is it really so hard for you to put yourself in Cleo's shoes?

OLIVIA: I'm not like her, Dad.

FRANK: Maybe one day you'll feel different.

OLIVIA: [*Scoffs.*] You think once I'm a mother, suddenly I'll have newfound respect for Cleo?

FRANK: From what I've seen, motherhood transforms women.

OLIVIA: It can deform them, too. Don't get your hopes up, Dad.

FRANK: My hopes are no higher than yours, Liv. [*Pause.*] When will you tell your mother about the baby?

OLIVIA: I don't know. They won't even let me see her.

FRANK: [*Extends his hand for her to hold.*] Come on. Let's try together. [*Liv hesitates, then takes her father's hand. He pulls her close and puts an arm around her shoulder as they head towards the house.*] I'm still on your side, you know. [*They approach the back door, try it, and find it open. They exit through house.*]

# ACT I

## Scene 4

[*The dining room of Cleo's cottage; the room is dim, smoky, candles are melted almost to the nubs. It is not a large or formal space; a long wooden table, draped in batik cloth, is surrounded by old, mismatched chairs. Seated in those chairs are the invited guests, who are laughing and feeling expansive now that the birthday feast is over. Liv stands in a corner, turning the camera on its tripod as each guest makes a toast or tribute to Cleo. Cleo sits in the center of the table, as Christ did at the Last Supper. She laughs, smiles, nods appreciatively as her friends and lovers pay tribute. The table is strewn with plates, bowls, wine glasses, and leftovers. When there is a lull in the conversation, Liv clears her throat to get the guests' attention.*]

OLIVIA: Excuse me, everyone. Could I have your attention, please? [*With help from Skye, the guests quiet down and wait for Liv to proceed.*] I know this is an unusual request, but I wondered if I could ask all of you to step outside for a moment. [*The guests make complaining sounds and Liv raises her voice to make a second appeal.*] It's a beautiful evening, and I'd really appreciate an opportunity to interview my mother, on the occasion of her sixtieth birthday, in private. [*Liv waits awkwardly for the guests to respond. Skye and Frank are the first to rise. Amy gathers Carter and also prepares to leave. The others look to Freda, who looks at Cleo. Cleo, never taking her eyes off of Liv, nods once and the others quietly leave. Liv, clearly nervous, fusses with the tripod in an attempt to move it closer to the table. Cleo watches her the entire time, patient but slightly bemused.*] It'll just take me a minute to set things up.

CLEO: [*Drags on a joint, filling her lungs and holding before blowing the smoke up towards the ceiling.*] Take your time.

[*Liv finally drags the tripod closer to her mother. The image on the view finder is projected onto the wall overhead. A second camera, offstage, projects Liv's image onto the wall as well. Unsure whether to sit or stand, Liv pulls out a chair, but only leans on its back.*]

OLIVIA: Ok, we're all set.

CLEO: [*Cleo looks at Liv expectantly, waiting for her to begin the interview. Liv says nothing, only adjusts the camera in minor ways while waiting for Cleo to begin.*] So. How does this work exactly?

OLIVIA: [*Confused, looks from camera to Cleo.*] Hm?

CLEO: [*Takes another drag then puts out the joint.*] Are you interviewing me, or am I just supposed to talk off the top of my head?

OLIVIA: Oh—uh…I thought we could just talk. You know—act like we're having a regular conversation. [*Cleo nods, but nevertheless waits for Liv to begin. There is an awkward silence.*] Um…why don't you tell me how it feels to turn sixty?

CLEO: [*Shrugs with her mouth.*] It's alright.

OLIVIA: When you were a young woman—or my age—could you have imagined your life turning out this way?

CLEO: I didn't think too much about the future back then.

OLIVIA: Why's that?

CLEO: It was out of my hands. I can only control the moment I'm in. The past and the future are beyond my reach.

OLIVIA: [*Playfully.*] Are you a Buddhist?

CLEO: I'm a realist.

OLIVIA: [*An awkward pause; Liv searches for common ground.*] This place—it's important to you.

CLEO: Yes.

OLIVIA: Some of your best plays were written in this house.

CLEO: You read my work?

OLIVIA: [*Caught off guard. She flushes, indignant.*] Of course.

CLEO: When I bought this house, it was really the land I was after. It was untouched—unmolested. I wanted you to grow up somewhere pure. The lake, the meadows, the trees…all of it fed my imagination. I hoped it would nourish you, too.

OLIVIA: Whenever I hear a cardinal, I think of this place. [*Relaxes and finally sinks into the chair.*] I have friends who've spent their entire lives in the city. I used to envy them, but now I pity them somehow. Jesse couldn't believe you lived all the way out here.

CLEO: Who's Jesse?

OLIVIA: [*Flushes deeply, stunned by her own carelessness.*] My husband.

CLEO: [*Regards Liv intently but says nothing for a moment.*] It's the quiet I love. Out here I remember the sound of my own silence. I need that silence in order to write.

OLIVIA: [*Hurt by Cleo's refusal to address her marriage, she becomes more formal.*] Can we talk about your decision to become a mother?

CLEO: [*Hesitates. Reaches for her glass, but it is empty. Liv grabs a pitcher of water and fills her mother's glass.*] Thanks.

OLIVIA: Do you mind talking about that now?

CLEO: [*Takes a long drink and clears her throat.*] Why not?

OLIVIA: If you know you need silence in order to create, why did you decide to have a child?

CLEO: I didn't know how loud you'd be. [*She smothers a grin by drinking once more.*] I thought I could handle it.

OLIVIA: Did that change once you got divorced? [*Cleo frowns, confused.*] You became a single parent when I was still in diapers. That must have been challenging.

CLEO: I wasn't single. I had Skye.

OLIVIA: And she had Amy.

CLEO: Right. We helped each other out. We were a family. A collective.

OLIVIA: Wouldn't a solitary life have been better?

CLEO: For whom?

OLIVIA: For your writing.

CLEO: I can't write in isolation. An artist needs community.

OLIVIA: But you just said you need silence.

CLEO: The right community can provide everything you need. If it doesn't, you build a new community.

OLIVIA: Is that why you left Skye?

CLEO: Technically, she left me. [*Pause.*] It was an amicable separation. She felt her poems couldn't blossom in my shadow.

OLIVIA: You haven't had a white lover since.

CLEO: That you know of. [*She enjoys Liv's surprise.*] You're not the only one with secrets.

OLIVIA: I wanted to tell you about Jesse…

CLEO: But?

OLIVIA: I guess I was afraid you'd be…disappointed.

CLEO: So you're a switch hitter, huh? [*Liv makes no reply.*] You love him?

OLIVIA: Yes.

CLEO: [*Shrugs, indifferent.*] Just remember you're responsible for your own happiness. It can't hinge on anyone else.

OLIVIA: What makes you happy, Cleo?

CLEO: [*She reflects for a moment.*] Power. Having a whim or an idea or an ambition, and then having everything I need to make it real.

OLIVIA: It must be frustrating, then, to be in your present… condition.

CLEO: "Condition"?

OLIVIA: [*Struggles to say the word aloud.*] Living with cancer.

CLEO: [*Stares at Liv, then drops her gaze.*] The way I see it, I'm still calling the shots.

OLIVIA: [*Mutters.*] Tell that to Freda.

CLEO: [*Laughs.*] Freda thinks you're an impudent brat. The spoiled fruit of my rotten womb.

OLIVIA: And what do you think?

CLEO: Well, Liv, you're what I would call…an acquired taste. It takes time to appreciate your…finer qualities.

OLIVIA: Mother love is supposed to be automatic.

CLEO: Don't believe the hype. Love is always a choice.

OLIVIA: Not when you're a child.

CLEO: Childhood doesn't last forever—thank God.

OLIVIA: I suppose you don't want any grandkids, then.

CLEO: You offering?

OLIVIA: [*Pause; switches back to her professional voice.*] Do you have any regrets? Anything you would do over?

CLEO: No.

OLIVIA: There's nothing in the past you wish you could change?

CLEO: I don't have time to imagine the impossible. I can't undo what's been done. I finished every project I began. That's what I set out to do. That's what I've done. This body may fail me, but my body of work will survive. [*Pause.*] What would you have me change?

OLIVIA: [*Hesitates, suddenly overcome. In a whisper.*] I wish…I wish we could have been friends.

CLEO: Mothers and daughters can never be friends.

OLIVIA: Why not?

CLEO: They're too much alike.

OLIVIA: We're not alike.

CLEO: [*Cleo laughs out loud, then quiets and observes her daughter.*] They're not equal, then.

OLIVIA: Growing up, I felt like your enemy.

CLEO: [*Grows somber.*] I didn't mean for you to feel that way. I always hoped Skye would be able to give you…whatever I couldn't.

OLIVIA: Skye was great. But she wasn't mine.

CLEO: You never met my mother.

OLIVIA: No.

CLEO: She was a hard woman to love.

OLIVIA: So why name me after her?

CLEO: Every time I tried to get close to her, my mother spat me out like I was a bad taste at the back of her mouth. I married Frank just to please her, but it wasn't enough. I decided to cut all ties with her just a month before she died. When you were born, I named you Olivia so I'd have a chance to call her name again.

OLIVIA: Didn't you want to be better than her?

CLEO: I like to think I was. You used to look at me like I was God.

OLIVIA: I was afraid of you. Afraid I'd do something so bad you'd send me away for good. You never cried when I went to stay with Dad.

CLEO: Why should I cry? I knew you'd be coming back in six months' time.

OLIVIA: Back then I thought…you were happy to get rid of me.

CLEO: [*Pause.*] Maybe I was. Raising a child—even with help—it's hard on the nerves. You try to anticipate every need, but you always fall short. Sometimes you have more to give, but you hold back—you hoard your time, your energy, your sympathy. You'll even let it rot just so you don't *have* to give it away. [*Pause.*] That sounds awful, doesn't it?

OLIVIA: Maybe you shouldn't have had any kids.

CLEO: Making a baby was the ultimate creative endeavor. I was so proud of myself when you were born! But as you grew, you became so…willful. You were the one project I couldn't truly complete. I couldn't make revisions—I couldn't tear up what I had and start over. I discovered you weren't really mine after all. But I was naïve then. I thought a child would be utterly devoted to me…forever.

OLIVIA: That's what you wanted from me—devotion?

CLEO: Motherhood is a betrayal. It's an illusion—a fantasy. We all go into it blind, and then the veil is torn…and we find ourselves at odds with our own image.

OLIVIA: You see yourself when you look at me?

CLEO: I do, but I don't. I do, but the mirror lies. You're a reflection that refuses to follow my commands. A shadow I can't step away from.

OLIVIA: So I betrayed you by being myself, and not some mindless clone.

CLEO: I tried to wean you, but you just kept holding on. You took my name.

OLIVIA: I'm your daughter!

CLEO: You're Frank's child, too. What was wrong with his name?

OLIVIA: I needed a way to show you…my allegiance. I wanted to be seen as a part of you. I was a teenager and—you kept pushing me away!

CLEO: So you took my name—my fame—and what did you give me in return? [*Liv is silent.*] Are you proud of that film?

OLIVIA: Yes, I am.

CLEO: [*Starts to speak, but chokes. With difficulty, she sips the water in her glass. Liv pours her some more, but Cleo waves her off.*] On the counter—by the fridge. There's a bottle—get it for me. [*Liv rises, and moves to the adjacent kitchen. The counter is covered with tinctures and herbal remedies.*]

OLIVIA: [*Panics, grabs each bottle and examines the handwritten label.*] Which one? There are dozens of bottles!

CLEO: [*Still coughing and sputtering.*] It's black—with a blue label.

OLIVIA: Got it! [*Liv rushes back over to the table and hands the bottle to Cleo, who refuses to take it.*]

CLEO: Put ten drops in here. [*She holds out her glass, which is half full of water. Liv counts out the drops, and then seals the bottle as Cleo swirls and then drains the contents of her glass. After a moment, the coughing subsides.*]

OLIVIA: Better? [*Cleo nods and settles back in her seat. Liv sees her mother's fatigue and decides to end the interview. She rises and presses the button to stop recording.*]

CLEO: [*Hoarse and weak but alert.*] What are you doing?

OLIVIA: We should probably stop now.

CLEO: Why?

OLIVIA: You look tired, Cleo. It's been a long day.

CLEO: [*Firmly.*] I'll stop when I'm ready to stop.

OLIVIA: [*Stops dismantling the camera and regards Cleo. Seeing her determination, Liv presses record once more and sits back down.*] Where were we?

CLEO: Why did you make that film?

OLIVIA: Why do you write any of your plays? Sometimes the words within us need to come out.

CLEO: I never put you in my plays.

OLIVIA: Most people could see your plays and never know you even had a daughter.

CLEO: You need the world to know I was an awful mother?

OLIVIA: I need to get beyond that time in my life. It was painful—even traumatic. Keeping it inside—keeping it private hurt too much.

CLEO: So publicizing your hatred of me is cathartic?

OLIVIA: I don't hate you, Mom.

CLEO: Anyone who sees that film will think otherwise.

OLIVIA: I didn't set out to malign you. If I had known you were—

CLEO: What?

OLIVIA: I didn't know you were sick.

CLEO: What difference does that make? It takes years to make a film. Would you have stopped the whole process-or just waited until I was dead before you released it?

OLIVIA: No! I just…why didn't you tell me?

CLEO: I didn't think you cared. You made it very clear in your last letter that you were done with me.

OLIVIA: I wrote that letter a year ago—I was upset! You said some terrible things, too, Cleo.

CLEO: Maybe I did. And now I'm dying. Happy? In a couple of months, this cancer will do what your precious little film couldn't.

OLIVIA: [*Starts to cry.*] I'm sorry! Ok? I'm sorry I made the film, I'm sorry I betrayed you. God—I just wanted you to be—

CLEO: What? Perfect?

OLIVIA: Proud. [*Tries to keep herself together but mostly fails.*]

CLEO: [*Yields before her daughter's distress.*] I've always been proud of you, Liv. I was proud the moment I laid eyes on you—just because you existed. Just because you made it here on your own.

OLIVIA: I know I've disappointed you…

CLEO: You're strong willed. Even as a child, I'd put you one place and you'd head somewhere else. I never could contain you, you'd just go your own way. [*Pause.*] It drove me crazy sometimes, but I've always admired that about you. It's why we had kids—to make a new generation, to keep the revolution going.

OLIVIA: But we aren't radical enough—or grateful enough. Are we?

CLEO: You were…once. You and Amy were raising hell before you even got to college. You broke every rule, crossed bridges we thought we'd burned. You seemed to learn from our mistakes. And then… [*She shrugs.*]

OLIVIA: Skye said you all were wondering where you went wrong.

CLEO: We were mourning the revolution. This isn't the world we wanted you to inherit. We weren't just fighting for ourselves, you know. Maybe you don't know. We wanted you to have the things we never had. But there's no real hunger without deprivation. We meant for you to be confident, not comfortable.

OLIVIA: Why can't we be both?

CLEO: Because comfortable women don't rock the boat—they support the status quo, and we don't have time for that. The world's going to hell in a hand basket, or hadn't you noticed? Maybe you're too preoccupied with your own pressing problems.

OLIVIA: The personal is political, right?

CLEO: Only if you use your personal experience to raise public consciousness.

OLIVIA: [*Shyly.*] I am working on a new script. [*Cleo frowns but says nothing.*] It's about two women—

CLEO: [*Dryly.*] Mother and daughter?

OLIVIA: No. One's an American soldier and the other's a so-called terrorist—a young Muslim woman who's considering suicide. It's a consideration of the value of martyrdom.

CLEO: [*Surprised and impressed.*] Hm. Sounds promising.

OLIVIA: Maybe—if you have time—maybe you could take a look at what I've got so far.

CLEO: [*Touched.*] Sure, Liv.

OLIVIA: [*Beams, but notices Cleo's strength is fading. The other guests become restless.*] I guess we should wrap this up. What advice would you give a young artist?

CLEO: Take risks. Build community. And defend what you believe.

OLIVIA: [*Wants desperately to reveal her pregnancy, but can't.*] What advice would you give to a woman artist about motherhood?

CLEO: [*Observes her daughter closely.*] There isn't one rule for all women. What works for some might not work for others.

OLIVIA: What advice would you give *me*?

CLEO: Give yourself room to grow along with your child. Stay open to the changes that will come and let go of the life you once had—because resistance *is* futile. Stay awake: don't try to live in a dream. And most importantly, forgive yourself when you fail. Because we all fail as mothers, in our own way. [*Pause.*] How far along are you?

OLIVIA: [*Fights back tears.*] Not far enough. [*The two women sit in silence for a moment. The camera beeps, indicating the cassette's almost finished. Liv stands and turns the camera off.*]

CLEO: I think I'm ready to turn in now. [*She groans as she tries to rise. Liv rushes around the table and helps her mother to stand. Cleo cannot walk alone, but is ashamed to admit it.*] Freda usually helps me into bed.

OLIVIA: I can help you…if you tell me what to do.

CLEO: [*Looks into her daughter's face.*] Alright. [*Cleo awkwardly turns and leans on Liv. The two slowly shuffle offstage. A moment later, Freda enters. She glances at the camera, then starts tidying up the mess on the table. She freezes when she sees the black bottle with blue label. She looks offstage, in the direction Cleo has gone, then pockets the bottle and continues clearing the table. Two other women enter to help her.*]

## **ACT II**

### **Scene 1**

[*The cabin occupied by Amy and Liv. Both women are still sleeping, but wake when vigorous pounding threatens to break down the door. Amy immediately goes to soothe Carter while Liv rubs her eyes and pulls back the curtain on the door.*]

OLIVIA: What the hell? [*Liv opens the door and confronts Freda standing behind two police officers.*]

COP 1: Are you Olivia Banks?

OLIVIA: What's going on?

FREDA: That's her!

COP 1: I'm going to have to ask you to get dressed and come with me, Miss.

OLIVIA: What? Why?

COP 1: We're investigating a possible homicide—

AMY: Homicide!

FREDA: She killed her! I saw it with my own eyes!

OLIVIA: Shut up, you crazy bitch! I'm not going anywhere until somebody tells me what's going on.

AMY: [*Comes forward, nursing Carter, and attempts to speak to the officer. Shamed, he looks away.*] Officer, if you would just explain why you're here…

COP 1: We've got a body up at the main house—a Cleo Banks—and this woman called the police. She says you poisoned her-uh-friend.

OLIVIA: My mother's dead?

FREDA: You killed her! You killed her!

[*Cop 2 leads Freda away from the door, attempting to calm her down.*]

AMY: Oh, Liv!

OLIVIA: [*Sinks onto the bed, stunned.*] Cleo's dead?

COP 1: [*Not unkind.*] I'm very sorry, Miss. But if you could just dress and come with me.

AMY: Where are you taking her?

COP 1: To the station.

AMY: [*Places Carter in his carrier and pulls some clothes on over her pajamas. She then turns to Liv, and offers her some clothes to put on as well. Turns to the officer.*] Do you mind? We just need a minute. [*Cop 1 hesitates, then steps back across the threshold so that Amy can close the door.*]

AMY: Come on, Liv. Put these on, and then we'll go find my mom. She'll know what to do. [*As if in a dream, Liv dons the clothes given to her. Amy collects Carter, and opens the cabin door. The officer nods, allows Amy to pass by first, then takes hold of Liv's arm and leads her away.*]

## ACT II

## Scene 2

[*The dining room of the cottage. The table has been cleared since last night, and now only holds the numerous empty wine bottles consumed during the dinner. The two friends of Cleo are in the room. One stares out a window, the other is slumped in a chair at the table. The mood in the room is somber. The door opens, and Skye enters, pleading with Cop 1. Still holding Liv by the arm, he directs her to sit at the table. Amy follows with Carter. Frank enters next, arguing with Cop 2 and Freda.*]

COP 1: [*Harassed by Skye and Amy.*] Ladies—ladies, please! [*Finally, there is silence.*] We are here on official police business. I appreciate that this is—a difficult time for everyone. But please—just let us do our job. [*He takes Liv's arm once more and pulls her up from the chair. Liv is numb, passive.*]

SKYE: But, officer, you don't understand—you're making a mistake! Liv loves her mother. She'd never do anything—

FREDA: She did it! I saw her! Murderer! [*Skye loses her temper and tries to throttle Freda. The two other women become involved, and the men attempt to pull them apart.*]

COP 2: If you don't calm down, you're all going to be under arrest!

SKYE: You can't arrest us—you don't have a warrant! [*The two women who a moment ago were fighting Skye, now back her up—* "Yeah!"; "Pig!"]

COP 2: I don't need a warrant to arrest you for disorderly conduct. Or for that marijuana you got growing out back. Now settle down!

FRANK: Officer, I'm Frank Edmunds, Olivia's father and her attorney. You must tell me why you're detaining my daughter.

COP 1: We have a complaint against her, sir. This woman claims Miss Banks, Sr. was murdered.

FREDA: Poisoned! And I have the proof. See—see this? [*She produces the black bottle with blue label.*] I found it there, on the table. She made all of us leave her alone, and then she killed Cleo!

OLIVIA: [*Finally starts paying attention. She looks at the bottle in Freda's hand.*] That? Mom told me to get it—she was choking—she said to put ten drops in her glass.

FREDA: Ten drops? Murderer!

FRANK: [*To Olivia.*] Liv, are you sure Cleo asked you to give her this—what is it, anyway? [*All eyes turns to Freda, who suddenly shrinks from the attention.*]

FREDA: Essence of snakeroot.

COP 2: What's it for?

FREDA: It is used to strengthen the womb. I gave it to Cleo—in small doses—after the chemo.

COP 1: Are you a doctor? [*Liv scoffs but is hushed by Frank.*]

FREDA: No.

COP 2: You got some kind of license for this?

FREDA: I am a traditional healer. I was trained in the old ways. I don't need no piece of paper tell me what to do.

COP 2: That's not the point. You're claiming this woman poisoned someone, and yet the poison belongs to you. [*He turns to Liv.*] Did anyone see you give this "essence" to your mother?

OLIVIA: No, we were alone.

SKYE: Yes! There is a witness! Your camera, Liv—where is it?

OLIVIA: In the cabin. [*Skye turns to Amy, who hands Carter to her mother and rushes out of the cottage.*]

SKYE: We can clear all this up, officer. Liv was filming her mother last night.

COP 1: And you got that on tape?

OLIVIA: I think so.

COP 2: [*Wanders over to counter and begins inspecting bottles.*] What else you got lying around? Maybe we should get a haz-mat crew out here.

FREDA: [*Rushes over to defend her tinctures.*] Don't touch them! These are natural oils, tinctures, and such, grown and gathered from this land. I have done nothing wrong. It is she who has broken the law—man's law and God's law! That one has brought nothing but grief to her mother—and now death!

OLIVIA: She told me to give it to her—I wouldn't do anything to hurt Cleo—

FRANK: Don't say anything, Liv.

[*Amy returns, breathless, holding Liv's black camera bag. She offers it to Liv, but COP 1 seizes it instead.*]

COP 1: This is coming with us.

SKYE: What? Why can't you look at it here, now? She's innocent!

FRANK: Don't worry, Skye. I'm going with her.

COP 2: [*To Cop 1.*] We can't leave without the body.

COP 1: Did you call for a bus?

COP 2: Yeah, but how're they going to get a gurney up here?

COP 1: Christ, what a mess...

SKYE: If you have time, officer, why not take a look at the tape?
[*The two cops exchange glances and decide they might as well. Cop 1 unzips the camera bag and removes the camera. He attempts to replay the tape, but must ask Liv for assistance. She takes the camera from him and puts it in replay mode. Skye, Freda, Amy, and Frank gather around the cops to watch. We hear the sound of Cleo coughing and the order that absolves Liv. Skye, Frank, and Amy sigh with relief and step back. Freda continues watching the tape over Liv's shoulder until one of the other women pulls her away.*]

COP 2: Well.

COP 1: [*Steps away from Liv.*] Sorry for the misunderstanding, Miss.

COP 2: The deceased will still have to be taken down to the morgue.

SKYE: What for?

COP 2: An autopsy will have to be performed.

SKYE: But it was—the tape proves that—

FREDA: Cleo wanted to die. [*She sinks into a chair, stunned.*]

SKYE: What?

FREDA: Cleo knew how potent snakeroot could be. I only ever gave her one drop at a time—two at most.

OLIVIA: [*Becomes hysterical as she understands what she's done.*] But she said *ten*! You heard her—she said *ten*! [*Frank and Skye exchange glances. Frank puts his hand on Liv's shoulder to steady her. Amy draws closer to Skye.*]

COP 1: Had Ms. Banks expressed her intention to…take her own life?

FREDA: Never—not to me. She wanted to fight—she wanted to live!

SKYE: [*To the cops.*] Cleo was losing her battle with cancer. She was in a lot of pain.

FREDA: She wasn't! We were managing the pain.

COP 2: With snakeroot?

FREDA: [*Quietly.*] With morphine. The doctor gave us a prescription. I did the best I could, but…she needed something stronger.

COP 1: [*Looks out window.*] It looks like they made it. I'll show them where the body is. [*He exits.*]

FREDA: [*Stands, alarmed.*] No! You can't take her. Cleo wanted to be buried here.

COP 2 : The body's going to the morgue, ma'am. You can arrange for it to be sent to the funeral home after the autopsy's been performed.

FREDA: [*With growing emotion.*] No! No! No funeral home! She wanted to die naturally—she wanted to be buried here, on this land—her land!

COP 2: I'm afraid you need a permit for that, ma'am. But for now, we got to go…[*He tries to extricate himself from her grasp and succeeds, but Freda follows him. The two other women join the chorus and follow Cop 2 out of the room.*]

SKYE: [*Watches them leave, then turns to the others.*] Well…

[*Frank hugs Liv, who then sinks into a chair. Amy peeks into Carter's carrier, then sits next to Liv and puts a hand on her arm.*]

OLIVIA: Thanks—all of you. I didn't even think of the camera.

SKYE: It's hard to think clearly under circumstances like these.

FRANK: [*Hears chaos offstage.*] Perhaps I should…go with the body.

SKYE: Would you?

FRANK: [*Nods at Skye, and squeezes Liv's shoulder.*] Will you be alright, baby? [*Liv pats her father's hand and nods. Frank exits. Amy and Skye exchange glances. Both notice Liv's growing distress.*]

SKYE: Why don't you go lie down, Liv?

AMY: I'll keep Carter up here for a while. You can have the cabin to yourself.

OLIVIA: Why did she do it? Why did she make *me* do it?

SKYE: Oh, Liv.

OLIVIA: Why not Freda? Why not you?

SKYE: It wasn't personal, Liv. She couldn't have planned this. Cleo didn't even know you were coming this weekend.

AMY: Cleo probably knew Skye and Freda would never help her kill herself.

OLIVIA: But I would?

SKYE: You were tricked, Liv—Cleo didn't want you to know…

OLIVIA: My own mother used me to commit suicide!

SKYE: It shows that Cleo trusted you, Liv…

OLIVIA: Trusted me? Sure—to be a complete fool. Boy, she's good…

AMY: Liv—

OLIVIA: I took your advice, Amy—I went easy on her. I told her how I really felt and—and I thought we were finally starting to connect. She even offered to read my script...[*Laughs cruelly.*] God—I'm such an idiot! She was just stringing me along.

SKYE: Cleo didn't have much time left, Liv.

OLIVIA: She had more than a few hours! She had weeks—maybe even months.

AMY: She was hurting, Liv.

OLIVIA: So am I! I'm hurting, too. [*Her rage dissolves into grief.*] All I wanted was another chance...

[*Skye folds Liv in her arms. Amy goes to join them, but Carter wakes and cries so she goes to him instead.*]

## ACT II

### Scene 3

[*A grassy knoll. A simple boulder marks Cleo's grave beneath a stately oak tree. Bunches of wildflowers have been left in honor of Cleo, suggesting the funeral service has only recently ended. Frank and Skye stand alone at the grave, holding hands.*]

FRANK: I never imagined I would lose her this way. But Cleo always was unpredictable.

SKYE: I think we're lucky. [*Frank looks at her quizzically.*] We knew her better than most. We loved her more...

FRANK: We knew her when...

SKYE: [*Drops his hand and grows bitter.*] God...Is this the best we can do? Uttering meaningless platitudes at the grave of our dead lover? [*Frank makes no reply.*] Cleo should have fought for her life. If not for her own sake, then for Liv's.

FRANK: I've been thinking…maybe Cleo felt her death would mean more to Liv.

SKYE: What?

FRANK: Maybe she just wanted to get out of the way so Liv could finally stand in the light.

SKYE: I hate to speak ill of the dead, Frank, but you and I both know Cleo wasn't that considerate. Especially not when it came to Liv.

FRANK: You're right. But—maybe I just need to see it this way— I'd like to think she meant this as a gift. Cleo made it to 60. She made amends with her only child.

SKYE: And she was surrounded by the people who loved her best. Maybe she did plan it after all. [*Pause. Skye gazes across the meadow as if looking at someone in the distance.*] I don't know if Liv will ever recover from this.

FRANK: Give her time. She'll heal.

SKYE: Death forces us to accept the permanence of things. Life is ephemeral but once it ends, some things cease to evolve. Anything *in utero* perishes as well.

FRANK: Is that poetry or philosophy?

SKYE: I don't have the right language for what I'm trying to say. I think Liv will stop grieving for Cleo eventually. But I suspect she'll always mourn the hope that died along with her. We just buried her last chance at having a better relationship with her mother.

FRANK: Liv showed me the tape—the complete interview with Cleo. They seem to have reached an understanding. I think they finally found common ground.

SKYE: And now Cleo's beneath it, leaving Liv alone.

FRANK: She has us. She has Jesse.

SKYE: [*Annoyed.*] Where is he, anyway?

FRANK: Off trying to make himself scarce. Liv told him she wanted to be alone.

SKYE: I suppose you sympathize?

FRANK: [*Nods knowingly.*] Yes, I do.

SKYE: You know, Frank. When Cleo left you—it wasn't personal.

FRANK: We don't have to do this, Skye. I made peace with the divorce thirty years ago.

SKYE: You were just a casualty in the war we had to fight to become our true selves. And for Cleo—a young black lesbian, rejected by her family, spurned by her community—you represented a kind of safety she couldn't find anywhere else.

FRANK: Until she met you.

SKYE: I couldn't protect Cleo from anything. But there is strength in numbers, and we felt secure in our love for one another. But there's a reason we moved up here and carved a life out of this wilderness. It wasn't only our desire to be closer to nature.

FRANK: Love is always a risk. When I married Cleo, I never imagined she'd leave me for another woman—and a white woman, at that! But I knew I could get hurt. I gave her my heart...she gave me Liv.

SKYE: This boy—Jesse. You like him?

FRANK: He's a grown man, Skye.

SKYE: He's not even thirty!

FRANK: Well, Liv thinks he's mature enough and I like him for her. But as I told him on their wedding day, he's got a long row to hoe. Those Banks women...they're beautiful, creative, but their heads are harder than stone.

SKYE: Men just can't handle a woman who knows her own mind.

FRANK: That's where you're wrong, Skye. Most men don't want to control women—they just want to be part of the plan.

SKYE: Oh, God! I get so tired hearing about how men feel left out...you marginalized women for thousands of years! You *need* to feel what it's like to not take center stage.

FRANK: Why can't you share the spotlight? Why do you have to leave us in the shadows?

SKYE: You're still bitter, aren't you? After all these years—"and a white woman, at that!"

FRANK: I'm not bitter. I'm simply asking a question. You two moved up here, you started this—women's commune. You built a world that had no place for men.

SKYE: So? You live in a black neighborhood—one of your daughters goes to Spelman!

FRANK: It's not the same—

SKYE: Of course, it is! You reserve the right—as a black man—to design a life that excludes whites.

FRANK: *I* didn't design segregation!

SKYE: No, but when it ended—when the civil rights movement gave you a new set of options—you looked around and still chose to live with your own kind. With people who affirm you—who respect your basic humanity.

FRANK: I don't hate white people.

SKYE: And I don't hate men. You limit your contact with your oppressor, and I do the same with mine.

FRANK: Can we ever be anything other than the enemy?

SKYE: Sure! One of my best friends is a man…[*She turns to go.*] I'm going to go check on Liv.

FRANK: She said she wanted to be left alone.

SKYE: That's what she told Jesse. [*Skye exits in search of Liv. Frank watches her go, frustrated by the abrupt end of their debate.*]

FRANK: And I suppose there's a different set of rules for you?

JESSE: [*Enters and hears Frank talking to himself.*] Sir?

FRANK: Oh—hello, son.

JESSE: Were you praying? I can leave, if—

FRANK: No, no, I was just muttering to myself. I'm glad you're here. I could use an ally. [*He smiles at Jesse.*] I could swear my testosterone level drops whenever I come up here.

JESSE: It's nice and peaceful, though.

FRANK: [*Smiles at his seeming innocence.*] It can be.

JESSE: Have you seen Liv?

FRANK: I think she's out by the lake. [*To deter Jesse from looking for her.*] Skye just went to check on her.

JESSE: Oh.

FRANK: So I understand you're going to be a father. Congratulations, son.

JESSE: Thank you, sir. We're really excited about the baby. I've always wanted to have kids. Liv wasn't so sure at first, but now I think she's really committed to the idea of becoming a mother.

FRANK: Well, it's more than a notion, raising a child. It's a lot of hard work. And Liv…Liv will need your help more than ever now.

JESSE: It's messed up, you know. Liv came here to tell Cleo that we'd gotten married and were having a baby. And instead she wound up burying her mother.

FRANK: In this family, you've got to learn to expect the unexpected.

JESSE: That funeral was something else!

FRANK: Well, Cleo wasn't religious in the traditional sense of the word. She practiced a kind of alternative spirituality.

JESSE: I didn't mind the chanting or holding hands—that part was cool. But I didn't expect there to be an all-out brawl…

FRANK: Oh, that. Well, Skye and Freda don't really get along. The weekend's been full of accusations, and…I guess emotions just boiled over. [*He glances at Jesse and tries to gauge his trustworthiness.*] It's ironic. These women pride themselves on being nothing like men, yet their egos are just as competitive, just as demanding.

JESSE: Yeah. When you strip away the trappings of gender—the ways we're socialized to perform masculine or feminine roles—you realize we're all just flawed human beings. [*Frank looks at Jesse, eyebrows raised.*] I minored in Women's Studies at college.

FRANK: Really?

JESSE: Um hmm. I also started a group on campus for pro-feminist men.

FRANK: You're a feminist?

JESSE: Well, it's not really appropriate for me to claim that title—it could be seen as an act of aggression. You know, men trying to colonize the women's movement. So we call ourselves pro-feminist instead, to show that we support the basic principles of feminism.

FRANK: [*Scrutinizes Jesse to gauge his sincerity. There is something about his speech that sounds as though it was learned by rote.*] I see. I'm starting to understand why my daughter married you, son.

JESSE: We do share similar politics, and we have the same artistic ambition. But I also love your daughter very much, sir. If I weren't already a pro-feminist man when we met, I'd have become one.

FRANK: Just to please her?

JESSE: Just to be worthy of her. I've learned so much about the condition of women...I'm actually hoping our first child's a girl.

FRANK: [*Whistles.*] Another Banks woman let loose upon the world...I'm hoping for a boy.

JESSE: To carry on the family name?

FRANK: Olivia doesn't bear my name.

JESSE: Oh, right. I forgot she'd changed it. Somehow I always think of you as one of them.

FRANK: I was never one of them.

JESSE: Well, maybe we'll be able to give you a grandson after all.

FRANK: I don't want a boy because I think they're better. No one here seems to understand that about me.

JESSE: I do. You want something different to add...balance to the family.

FRANK: [*Amazed at Jesse's accuracy.*] Yes, that it!

JESSE: Being pro-feminist doesn't mean I'm anti-male. I'd love to have a daughter *and* a son. What matters is giving your child permission to live outside your expectations. [*Pause. He glances across the meadow to where Liv sits with Skye. His tone becomes more earnest.*] I think Liv worries about being a good mother.

FRANK: She'll be fine.

JESSE: I keep telling her that, but...she's afraid of not being good enough.

FRANK: Aren't we all?

JESSE: Yeah, but it's different for today's women. They grew up being told they could do anything with their bodies.

FRANK: They can.

JESSE: It's a lot of pressure, though, having that power and knowing just what to do with it. We never have to think about juggling our priorities. No one will judge us if we put our careers ahead of our kids.

FRANK: A man's expected to provide for his family.

JESSE: A woman's expected to put her family first. But for many women, motherhood isn't enough. I think Liv is…ambivalent. She doesn't want to fail on either front.

FRANK: I thought the war was over.

JESSE: [*Shakes his head.*] Most men aren't willing to share the power they've got. And women now fight against their own ambition. They're caught between a rock and a hard place.

FRANK: So what can we do to help?

JESSE: Stand by them. Give them support without judgment, without telling them what to do.

FRANK: Maybe if I'd had your enlightened attitude, Cleo wouldn't have left me.

JESSE: Well, from what Liv's told me, Cleo didn't leave because of you. She just wanted a more authentic life.

FRANK: When you're with Liv, do you ever feel…useless?

JESSE: [*Glances across the meadow.*] Sometimes I want to be her focus. But I've learned to act like an adult in our relationship. I mean, it's childish, right? Wanting her only to think of me. [*They stand in silence for a moment, neither one convinced by the idea.*] We have to negotiate the terms of our relationship. As a lawyer, I'm sure you can appreciate the importance of reading the fine print—"terms and conditions apply."

FRANK: When I was your age, I thought love was supposed to be unconditional.

JESSE: It's a hard lesson to learn, but if you take her love for granted, you risk losing it all…you have to work for it, earn it every day. Liv's an independent woman. She already has a father. She already has a career. I just try to find my niche, my own unique role. And that can't just be based on what *I* want.

FRANK: [*Looks at Jesse, marveling at his maturity.*] Cleo would have liked you.

JESSE: I wish I could have met her before…[*Their gazes are drawn to the grave. Skye and Liv approach. They stop a few feet off, and Skye takes Liv's chin in her hands. She says something that seems like advice; they mime a gentle interrogation.*]

FRANK: Well, I'd better head back to the city. It's been real nice talking to you, son.

JESSE: [*Shakes Frank's hand.*] My pleasure, sir. I hope we get to see more of each other in the months to come.

FRANK: Count on it. This old fool has a lot left to learn, and you might be just the man to teach me. [*Skye enters, leading Liv who is somber. Frank reaches for Liv.*] Baby. [*He kisses her forehead and looks into her face.*] I'm going to go now. But I'm leaving you in some very capable hands. [*Skye smiles, then realizes Frank is referring to Jesse. Frank takes Liv's hand, and places it in Jesse's.*] You two take care of each other.

JESSE: We will, sir.

[*Frank nods at Skye, then exits.*]

SKYE: Well. [*She is clearly reluctant to leave them alone, but can find no reason to stay. Liv is impassive, barely responding to Jesse's attempts to comfort her.*] Amy will be leaving soon, too. I'd better go see if she needs a hand with the baby. [*To Liv, pointedly.*] You remember what I told you. [*Liv nods. Skye exits without ever acknowledging Jesse.*]

JESSE: We should probably head out soon, too. I lined up a few potential investors—I thought we could do lunch sometime this week… [*He waits for Liv to respond.*] …if you're up for it. Do you need more time?

OLIVIA: [*Dully.*] For what?

JESSE: I don't know. I thought maybe you felt closer to your mom out here.

OLIVIA: My mother's dead, Jesse.

JESSE: I know that, Liv. I'm just…I'm asking you to tell me what you need right now.

OLIVIA: What if I don't know what I need?

JESSE: Then let me take you home. [*He tries to embrace her, but she eludes him.*]

OLIVIA: [*She kneels beside the grave.*] Everything's changed, Jess.

JESSE: [*He squats next to her and strokes her hair.*] You need time to adjust. Remember when my grandmother died? At first the loss seemed unbearable, but you helped me get through it. And I'm going to be here for you, Liv.

OLIVIA: Cleo named me after her mother.

JESSE: You never mentioned your grandmother before.

OLIVIA: I never met her. Cleo cut all ties with her before I was born. [*Jesse nods.*] Apparently my grandmother was a hard woman to love.

JESSE: I guess the fruit doesn't fall far from the tree.

OLIVIA: [*Shoots him a deadly glance.*] I guess not. [*Jesse senses the edge in her voice and tries to counter it with more tenderness.*]

JESSE: Let me take you home, Liv.

OLIVIA: [*Again, rejects his touch.*] What's the rush?

JESSE: There is no rush. I just want to take care of you, and I can't do that here.

OLIVIA: I can take care of myself, Jesse. I always have.

JESSE: Because you had to. You're not alone, Liv. [*She turns away from him.*] You have me. And the baby.

OLIVIA: [*She spins, snaps.*] *Fetus.*

JESSE: What?

OLIVIA: I'm six weeks pregnant, Jesse. It's not a baby yet.

JESSE: It will be one day. You're carrying our child.

OLIVIA: *Fetus.* It's a spec of life inside *my* body.

JESSE: Ok. But it's still a part of us—of you and me. Remember what the doctor said about how critical the first three months are. The baby—the fetus—needs to feel welcome. She or he can sense your emotions.

OLIVIA: Maybe I'll have a miscarriage then. [*Jesse stares at her, aghast.*] I can't manufacture bliss right now. Not for its sake—or yours.

JESSE: Of course, Liv. You're grieving, it's natural for you to be upset. But I hope you can see yourself as part of the cycle of life—every end signals a new beginning.

OLIVIA: Why recycle dysfunction? Some cycles need to just stop.

JESSE: You can't stop life, Liv. [*She makes no reply, but they both know that he is wrong. Unable to accept Liv might be considering an abortion, Jesse tries to change the topic.*] Why don't we go away for a few days—just the two of us?

OLIVIA: [*Stands.*] We don't have time—or money—for a vacation. I just want to get on with my life.

JESSE: Ok. Ok. We'll do that then. Sometimes carrying on is the best way to get beyond grief. [*Liv turns to go. Jesse hesitates, then grabs her hand and forces her to look at him.*] Liv—have you...[*He pleads with her with his eyes, but Liv will not respond.*] Have you changed your mind about the baby?

OLIVIA: [*Cannot look him in the eye.*] I learned some things about myself this weekend. Things I didn't want to admit before.

JESSE: Like?

OLIVIA: Like how desperate I've been to prove myself to Cleo.

JESSE: That's only natural, considering your...history. Everyone wants their parents' approval, Liv.

OLIVIA: Oh yeah? Well, you can't prove anything to a corpse. [*Pause.*] Desperate people do desperate things, Jesse. They aren't always rational.

JESSE: There's nothing irrational about wanting a child.

OLIVIA: [*She turns away.*] I don't know what I want.

JESSE: But...[*He tries to balance his understanding of "the condition of women" with his own desire.*] What's changed? You were so happy just a few days ago—you couldn't wait to tell everyone.

OLIVIA: Not everyone—Cleo.

JESSE: So what happened? Did she try to change your mind?

OLIVIA: No! No. She just—she helped me see myself in a different light. Cleo and I—we're more alike than I ever imagined.

JESSE: Liv—just because Cleo failed you as a mother, doesn't mean—

OLIVIA: [*She unconsciously begins quoting Cleo.*] Mothers always fail their daughters—it's inevitable.

JESSE: Inevitable? Liv, failure isn't encoded in your DNA!

OLIVIA: It might be! Look at the evidence—it doesn't point to success.

JESSE: But…this is about you, Liv—not your mother, or your grandmother.

OLIVIA: You said yourself—the fruit doesn't fall far from the tree.

JESSE: That's not what I meant.

OLIVIA: Cleo tried to be better than her mother, but she failed. I want to be better than Cleo, but chances are, I'll fail, too. I'm not cut out for motherhood—I'm too scattered, too selfish!

JESSE: You can change, Liv. A child might help you change.

OLIVIA: What if I can't balance having a kid and having a career? I'm a filmmaker, Jesse. All my creative energy goes into my work. I barely have enough left over for you! Don't tell me you don't feel neglected sometimes.

JESSE: You have more than enough love for me *and* a child, Liv.

OLIVIA: I'm not talking about love! I'm talking about my time, my energy, my need to put myself first. How can I become a mother when I know I'm a narcissist?

JESSE: What? That doesn't even make sense! A narcissist doesn't *know* she's a narcissist. That's the problem! [*He grabs her by the shoulders.*] YOU are self-aware, Liv. You know your strengths and weaknesses. You understand your own motives. I know you want this child.

OLIVIA: [*Avoids his gaze.*] It's my body, Jess.

JESSE: [*Drops his hands from her arms.*] What are you going to do—have another abortion?

OLIVIA: Don't say it like that.

JESSE: You're not that young, Liv. If you terminate this pregnancy, what are the odds we'll be able to conceive again?

OLIVIA: If it's meant to be, it'll happen.

JESSE: It already has happened. To both of us! This is my child, too, Liv.

OLIVIA: [*With less force.*] It's my body.

JESSE: Fine. We can adopt.

OLIVIA: I don't want to be a mother, Jesse!

JESSE: [*Pause.*] Do you still want to be a wife?

OLIVIA: [*Rushes to him.*] Oh, God, Jess—of course, I do! [*She embraces him tightly.*] I don't know what's wrong with me…so much has happened these past few days. I wasn't ready to stop being her daughter. [*Liv weeps softly and Jesse holds her tenderly.*] Take me home, Jess.

JESSE: Come on. Let's go get your bags.

OLIVIA: Everything's packed. Can I meet you at the cabin? I just need a moment alone.

JESSE: Sure, babe. Take your time. [*He kisses her and exits. Liv takes one last look at her mother's grave, then checks to see that Jesse is gone, and heads for Freda's studio.*]

## **ACT II**

## **Scene 4**

[*Freda's studio, which is in a converted barn. Large, colorful canvases rest again the raw wood-plank walls. An easel stands to one side; it displays a gorgeously painted portrait of Cleo. A wooden table covered with paint and supplies is nearby. Freda enters, carrying a small, full box and a larger, empty one. As she sets the smaller box on the table, we hear the rattle of glass bottles. Freda lets the larger box drop to the ground. She turns to look longingly at the portrait, and wipes tears from her eyes. Freda is about to exit the barn when Liv enters.*]

OLIVIA: [*Holds up her hands in mock surrender.*] I'm not looking for a fight. I just want to talk to you. [*Freda backs into the studio and turns away, wiping at her face. Liv enters the barn and looks at the art, her gaze resting on the portrait of Cleo.*] You're really talented. You've captured her completely. [*Freda accepts the compliment with a silent nod, and goes over to the table. She sets the empty box on the table and begins putting lids on her paints before placing them in the box.*] What are you doing?

FREDA: Packing.

OLIVIA: Why?

FREDA: You think I'm going to let you throw me out like a piece of trash?

OLIVIA: Where will you go?

FREDA: I have friends.

OLIVIA: What will you do with all your art?

FREDA: [*Stops fussing with items on the table and examines her large canvasses.*] I'll rent a truck and come back.

OLIVIA: You can't bring a truck up to the house. You know that.

FREDA: [*Searches for another solution.*] Then I'll leave them.

OLIVIA: [*Weighs the situation and sees a way to work it to her advantage.*] Listen, Freda. I know you don't think much of me, but I'm not a heartless bitch. I know you loved my mother…in your way. Just like I loved Cleo in my way. [*Freda eyes Liv with suspicion.*] You don't have to go.

FREDA: [*Defensively.*] I don't need your pity. And I won't stay where I'm not wanted.

OLIVIA: Freda, I don't want you to go.

FREDA: [*Suspiciously.*] Why?

OLIVIA: If you leave, the place will be empty—abandoned. And Cleo—she shouldn't be left alone. You were her companion, her caregiver—

FREDA: [*Defiant, proud.*] I was her lover.

OLIVIA: This is your home. You don't really want to go, do you?

FREDA: I've seen Cleo's will. This land, the house, and everything in it belongs to you now.

OLIVIA: Then I get to say what happens here, right? Well, I say you can stay.

FREDA: [*Touched, but still wary.*] What do you want from me?

OLIVIA: [*Glances at the portrait.*] You want to stay here, right?

FREDA: Yes.

OLIVIA: Then there are two things I need from you.

FREDA: [*Satisfied that Liv has ulterior motives, she folds her arms across her chest.*] What?

OLIVIA: [*Moves over to the portrait.*] This painting of my mother. [*Freda frowns, but holds her tongue. Liv admires the painting, tracing its outlines with her fingertips.*] I need you to give it to Skye.

FREDA: What? Never! I will never give anything to that woman! [*Olivia merely shrugs and wanders over to the box on the table. Freda fumes, but calms herself enough to ask a question.*] What else?

OLIVIA: Hm?

FREDA: You said you wanted two things.

OLIVIA: [*Lightly.*] Oh, right. [*Liv begins casually examining the bottles in Freda's box.*] I need you to give me one of your herbal remedies.

FREDA: [*Wary yet sarcastic.*] For what? Bellyache?

OLIVIA: You told that cop you were trained in the old ways.

FREDA: [*Proudly.*] My granny taught me everything she knew, and she was taught by her mother before her. A true Wampanoag shaman taught me the healing properties of the plants that are native to this land.

OLIVIA: [*Makes a face to show she's impressed.*] They say that back in the day, even during slavery, women knew how to purge the womb—naturally. Is that true? [*Freda stares at Liv for a moment then goes and takes the bottle from her hand. She positions herself so that her body is between Liv and the box of bottles.*]

FREDA: I wouldn't know. I'm a healer.

OLIVIA: You do what you do to help women, right? Well, I need your help.

FREDA: You're asking me to "help" you kill Cleo's own flesh and blood?

OLIVIA: [*Turns away, ashamed.*] I'm not fit to be a mother. You know that. You told Cleo I was nothing but a spoiled brat.

FREDA: [*Humbled.*] Spoiled fruit makes the sweetest cake. [*Liv looks at her, confused.*] Sometimes the worst daughters make the best mothers.

OLIVIA: Some women shouldn't have kids. Ever.

FREDA: Your mother died trying to save her womb.

OLIVIA: I want to keep my uterus. Just—

FREDA: --not the child inside.

OLIVIA: [*Decides not to prolong the conversation.*] Look, I'm leaving in about twenty minutes. Do we have a deal? [*Freda deliberates.*]

FREDA: I'll meet you up at the house. [*Liv tries to conceal her relief. She exits, and Freda removes a mortar and pestle from the box. She is about to leave to gather the roots she needs, when Cleo's portrait gives her pause. Freda stands for a moment, transfixed. Then she removes the painting from the easel, leans it face down against the other canvases, and rushes from the barn.*]

## ACT II

## Scene 5

[*The front of Cleo's cottage, where the play began. Jesse stands to one side, surrounded by Liv's bags. Skye and Liv descend the porch steps, arms around each other's waist.*]

SKYE: Are you sure you won't stay another night? With Amy gone, you and Jesse could have the cabin to yourselves.

OLIVIA: We really need to get back. You take the cabin—it's probably best if you and Freda don't sleep under the same roof tonight. [*Skye makes a face and Liv decides to own up to her "deal."*] I told her she could stay.

SKYE: Here? For how long?

OLIVIA: As long as she wants. Someone needs to be here, and my life is in the city. [*Skye acts petulant.*] How long are you planning to stay?

SKYE: Just one more night. I need to get back to my own place. I've got a reading at the public library next week.

OLIVIA: [*Nods and pretends to scold Skye.*] So—I can count on you not to cause any more drama, right?

SKYE: The kids in my poetry class have a saying: "Don't start nothin' won't be nothin'." It works better than the Golden Rule. [*They smile and then embrace.*] Take care of yourself, Liv. And keep in touch.

OLIVIA: I will, I promise. [*Jesse steps forward to hug Skye, who barely tolerates the embrace.*]

JESSE: [*To Liv.*] Ready? [*Liv nods but looks over her shoulder. Jesse prompts her to follow him, but at the last minute, Freda rushes up to the house. She is holding the portrait of Cleo in one hand and a blue bottle in the other. Liv faces Freda, expectant.*]

OLIVIA: You came! We have a deal then?

FREDA: [*Turns to Skye, purses her lips, and hands her the painting.*] Here. [*Freda doesn't wait to see Skye's response; she turns to Liv. Skye takes the painting and stands staring at it, mesmerized.*] You're sure this is what you want?

OLIVIA: [*Flushes, not wanting the others to witness their transaction.*] I'm sure.

FREDA: [*Hands the bottle to Liv.*] Two drops a day, until it's done.

OLIVIA: That's it?

FREDA: It takes time to accumulate in the blood. You must finish it all, understand? [*Liv nods, and pockets the bottle. She smiles and waves at Skye, who has become curious. Liv follows Jesse offstage. Freda and Skye stand by the porch, watching them depart.*]

SKYE: I don't know what to say, Freda.

FREDA: Then don't say a thing. [*She turns to go up the stairs but Skye stops her.*]

SKYE: Thank you. [*Freda merely nods. Skye holds the painting up to examine it, and for a moment they stand together, lost in their admiration and grief. Finally, Freda tears herself away. As she mounts the stairs, Skye calls to her again.*] Freda—what was that you gave Liv? In the blue bottle.

FREDA: She asked me to prepare a special tincture.

SKYE: [*Knowing.*] And you gave her what she asked for?

FREDA: [*Gives a slight, sly smile.*] I gave her what she needed.

SKYE: Pennyroyal?

FREDA: Snakeroot. To strengthen the womb. [*Freda goes up the stairs and enters the cottage. Skye considers Freda's words, and sits down on the steps. She props the painting beside her. Cleo's smile is enigmatic.*]

## THE END

# BEAST

## A Two-Act Play

by

Zetta Elliott

Copyright © 2007 Zetta Elliott

# BEAST

## Synopsis:

A family gathers at a ranch in Nevada to strategize and escape the media frenzy surrounding the only son. DeMarcus Gaines, a famous basketball player, has been implicated in a shooting that may end his career; these charges are just the latest in a string of accusations leveled against the young star, including rape. His family, from whom he has been estranged, decides to rally around DeMarcus, but only after he gives a full and honest account of his actions.

## List of Characters:

**DeMarcus:** a black male athlete in his mid-20s; he is strong yet lean, good-looking, charming, yet arrogant; he entered professional sports without going to college, and so seems immature at times; at other times, he is remarkably savvy, yet depends heavily on the advice of his agent/manager, Monty

**Diane:** doting mother of DeMarcus and wife of Alvin; in her early 60s.

**Dana:** eldest sister of DeMarcus; also a basketball player, Dana led her college team to the national championships, and went on to play in the WNBA; she is now coaching, and expecting a child with her lover, Lynn; Dana resents the attention her brother has always received and the shame he has brought on the family; she is 36.

**Deirdre:** second-eldest sister of DeMarcus; she runs her own hair salon and has two sons; she is divorced; although Deirdre resents men as a group, she adores DeMarcus but shares her sister's dislike of Mirlana; she is 34.

**Mirlana:** mixed-race woman in her early 20s; wife of DeMarcus; former dancer/stripper; mother of his two young daughters

**Alvin:** father of DeMarcus; a former athlete himself, Al devoted most of his life to ensuring his son's success as a professional athlete. However, once DeMarcus achieved star status, Al no longer had the same influence over his son, and broke all ties after DeMarcus' marriage to Mirlana. He has called the family together now, since DeMarcus' latest escapade threatens to end his professional career; he is in his mid-sixties.

**Monty:** a white man in his mid-30s; slick, shrewd; agent/manager of DeMarcus and unspoken rival of Alvin

## Setting:

A ranch in Nevada.

## Time:

Now.

## ACT I

## Scene 1

[*A large, recently updated kitchen. Diane moves from counter to stove to fridge, preparing DeMarcus' favorite meal. Deirdre sits at the breakfast bar, lazily chopping vegetables but mostly keeping her mother company.*]

DIANE: I wish I knew when they were coming.

DEIRDRE: Soon, Mom.

DIANE: How soon? The shrimp will keep, but the lobster—you know your brother likes it fresh…

DEIRDE: Leave it on ice. It's going to be at least a few more hours. When I talked to Marcus this morning, he said they were flying into Vegas and then driving the rest of the way.

DIANE: Flying? But that means he'll bring the reporters here!

DEIRDRE: Relax, Mom. Private jet. Tinted glass. Monty thought of everything.

DIANE: Oh. *He*'s not coming, is he?

DEIRDRE: I don't think so. Marcus said Monty had to meet with the attorneys. They're launching a suit against the league.

DIANE: [*Shakes her head and focuses on her cooking once more.*] There's something not quite right about that man…

DEIRDRE: [*Shrugs.*] I don't trust him, either, but you can't say he doesn't work for that million-dollar commission. If DeMarcus Gaines goes down, Monty goes down with him.

DIANE: Unless he sinks his fangs into some other rising star. The man's a leech.

DEIRDRE: You sound like Dad.

DIANE: Your father knows about these things. After all, he played in the same league—

DEIRDRE: Thirty years ago!

DIANE: [*Undeterred.*] --and he met his fair share of unscrupulous agents.

DEIRDRE: And Monty stole his job. Face it, Mom: Dad's bitter.

DIANE: He has a right to be. He dedicated the better part of his life to managing your brother's career.

DEIRDRE: Dad got Marcus noticed. But Monty made him a star.

DIANE: Well, Monty isn't family. Your brother needs us, Dee.

DEIRDRE: Right about now, Marcus needs all the help he can get.

DIANE: [*Becomes still.*] It's bad, isn't it.

DEIRDRE: [*Sighs.*] The bouncer at that club—he's paralyzed.

DIANE: Your brother doesn't even own a gun!

DEIRDRE: [*Frowns at her mother's naiveté.*] Marcus was there, Mom. In some way or other, he's involved…

DIANE: That boy's always in the wrong place at the wrong time…

DEIRDRE: [*Forces optimism.*] Well, things have looked bad before, and Marcus pulled through. If a black athlete can beat a rape charge, he can beat anything! [*Diane's face clouds and Deirdre wishes she hadn't mentioned the rape. Sounds of someone arriving offstage draw their attention. Diane brightens, hastily removes her apron, and tidies her hair. Deirdre smiles at her mother's anticipation, but both women are surprised when Dana enters instead of DeMarcus.*]

DIANE: [*Barely hides her disappointment.*] Oh. Dana. [*Feigns pleasure and gives her daughter a perfunctory kiss.*] We thought you were—

DANA: [*Sets down a large shopping bag and moves into the room.*] The son of God? Hasn't he returned yet to claim his throne? [*Diane shakes her head and turns away. She puts her apron back on and gives her attention to the pots.*] At least preparations for the Last Supper are well underway. [*Dana snoops around the stove and gets shooed away by her mother.*]

DEIRDRE: [*Gets off her stool to embrace her sister.*] Hey, Dane.

DANA: Hey, Dee. [*They share a meaningful, genuine embrace.*] Where are your little angels?

DEIRDRE: With Satan.

DIANE: [*Petulant.*] I don't see why the boys had to stay with Darnell this weekend.

DEIRDRE: [*For the tenth time.*] Because his mother's in town, and she wanted to see her grandkids.

DIANE: And I don't? I'm their grandmother, too.

DEIRDRE: You don't live in St. Croix.

DIANE: I don't see what that's got to do with anything.

DEIRDRE: You can see the boys anytime you want! Cut the woman some slack, Mom. She's already traumatized by the fact that she raised a dog instead of a man.

DANA: [*Dryly, to Diane.*] Surely you can sympathize with that. [*To Deirdre.*] I bought some things for the boys. You got room in your suitcase?

DEIRDRE: [*Glances at the bag Dana left by the door.*] The way you shop? Probably not.

DIANE: You spoil those boys rotten, Dana.

DANA: Ain't that the pot… [*She rolls her eyes and Deirdre snickers.*]

DIANE: [*Alarmed.*] Pot?

DEIRDRE: …calling the kettle black. She's being sarcastic, Mom.

DANA: Actually, I was being ironic. I hardly think you're in a position to lecture me about the danger of overindulging boys.

DIANE: [*Ignores the implication that she spoiled her son.*] Seems to me you could be putting all that energy into having your own kids by now. [*Deirdre senses danger and tries to change the subject.*]

DEIRDRE: Is Marcus bringing his girls?

DIANE: I certainly hope so. It's about time I met my granddaughters. And he's got to shield them from all this…hysteria!

DANA: Then he needs to shield them from himself—and that mother of theirs…

DEIRDRE: SHE isn't coming, is she?

DANA: Of course, she is! Marcus won't go anywhere without his precious wifey. After all, he's got an image to protect.

DEIRDRE: And nothing screams "wholesome" like having a stripper on your arm. [*The sisters snicker.*]

DIANE: [*Starts aggressively stirring or mashing the food.*] Mirlana is a *dancer*.

DANA: Sure, Mom. She "dances" around a pole wearing a sequined thong…

DIANE: That was before she met your brother!

DEIRDRE: Right. And since the wedding, she's been an upstanding model of female virtue.

DANA: Not that you can blame her, considering what Marcus has put her through. If I were her, I might be banging the pool boy, too. [*Diane loudly bangs a spoon against a pot. The sisters ignore her and continue to shred their sister-in-law.*]

DEIRDRE: Please. She knew what she was getting into…if you marry a baller, you're gonna get played.

DANA: Paid, you mean.

DEIRDRE: I still can't believe Marcus didn't make her sign a pre-nup.

DIANE: Your father never asked me to sign one. [*The sisters exchange glances and dissolve into laughter.*]

DANA: Oh, God, Mom—are you serious? They didn't even have pre-nups back then.

DIANE: Of course, they did!

DEIRDRE: Well, Dad wasn't worth 25 million when he popped the question.

DANA: Marcus has got to be worth ten times that now, even after losing those endorsements.

DIANE: Your father's love was priceless to me…[*The sisters smother their laughter to respect their mother's sentimentality.*] I didn't care how much he was "worth."

DANA: You and Dad were college sweethearts, Mom. Emphasis on "college."

DEIRDRE: Yeah, Mom. You can't compare yourself to Mirlana. She isn't fit to clean your house, no matter how cute she thinks she is.

DIANE: [*Sighs.*] Sometimes love is blind.

DANA: It must have been if Marcus didn't see the tattoo on Mirlana's ass—[*In unison with Deirdre.*] GOLDDIGGER!

DIANE: Nevertheless, she's part of the family now, and the mother of your two nieces. I expect you to treat your sister-in-law with respect this weekend… [*The sisters roll their eyes. Diane becomes stern.*] …and a little extra consideration.

DEIRDRE: Why should we be considerate of her? She barely gives us the time of day.

DIANE: This is a difficult time for Mirlana...

DANA: So tell Marcus to show her a little extra consideration!

DIANE: I just think your sister-in-law could use a little female sympathy right now.

DANA: Why? Is it that time of the month?

DEIRDRE: Mirlana's got permanent PMS, Mom. It'll take more than Midol to fix her bad mood. [*The sisters laugh.*]

DIANE: I didn't raise you to act like this. To look down your nose at other people.

DANA: Yes, you did! You made damn sure Dee and I didn't turn out anything like Mirlana.

DIANE: Not all girls had the benefit of your home training.

DEIRDRE: True! Marcus had to *pay* Mirlana's parents to leave them alone. Her father took that check and moved his family right back to Brazil.

DANA: Bolivia, you mean.

DIANE: Buenos Aires, I think.

DEIRDRE: Whatever! The point is, they basically sold their own daughter!

DANA: People pimp their children out all the time. [*She eyes her mother, who ignores her.*] These days, everything's for sale...even forgiveness. She still sporting that rock Marcus bought her before the trial?

DEIRDRE: All 8 carats...

DIANE: Alright, you two, that's enough! Marcus asked me not to tell you this, but—[*The sisters lean in, intrigued.*] Mirlana lost the baby.

DANA: Baby? She was pregnant—

DEIRDRE: —again? Damn! Must be that hot Latin blood...

DANA: She's not Latin—she's half-Indian, or something. Aztec.

DIANE: Pueblo, I think.

DEIRDRE: Whatever. How many kids does she need to have?

DANA: Do the math: alimony for her, plus child support for three kids!

DEIRDRE: [*Whistles.*] A hundred grand per month, easy. She's the ultimate welfare queen!

DIANE: I expected more from you, Dee.

DANA: [*Defensive.*] Why?

DIANE: Because she's a mother. You don't know how devastating a miscarriage can be. [*Dana's face clouds. Deirdre senses danger again.*]

DEIRDRE: I thought after all the trouble with the last pregnancy they decided not to have any more kids.

DIANE: Well, they went to see a fertility specialist—the best in the country—and he said everything would be alright…

DEIRDRE: I guess money can't buy everything after all. [*All three women are silent for a moment.*]

DIANE: Whatever you do, don't let on that you know about the baby. Just try to—be gentle with her. Remember, we're all on the same team.

DANA: God—I keep hoping I'll get drafted. Being on Team Marcus is more than I can stand…

DIANE: It's the GAINES team. Honestly, Dana, this sibling rivalry has got to stop! I know you've always resented your brother's success—

DANA: What I resent is having my good name dragged through the mud every time Marcus slides back into the gutter.

DIANE: Would it kill you to give him a hand up? You'd rather stand back and laugh at his misfortune.

DANA: Marcus isn't unlucky, Mom! He's made choices that are stupid and selfish—

DIANE: So what if he has? Are you perfect? I suppose you've never made a mistake!

DEIRDRE: [*Trying to diffuse the situation.*] We all make mistakes—

DANA: I take responsibility for the choices I've made in my life. Why shouldn't Marcus do the same?

DIANE: You don't know what it's like—fame does things to people.

DANA: You're right, Mom, it does. Fame makes people think they're invincible—untouchable—entitled to whatever they want, whenever they want it. Marcus is like a kid in a candy store, stuffing his mouth and his pockets with everything in sight. Yet when he pukes it up, you don't call him a glutton. And when the cops come around, you won't admit he's a thief. Face it, Mom—with Marcus, your amazing home training just didn't take.

DIANE: [*Torn between guilt, grief, and a desire to lash out at someone.*] You don't know what it's like—how a mother suffers when her child goes astray! [*Dana groans with disgust and Deirdre again tries to make peace.*]

DEIRDRE: Why don't we just wait until Marcus gets here. Let's hear what he has to say and then—

DANA: Then what, Dee? There isn't a band-aid big enough to cover his scrape this time.

DEIRDRE: You said it yourself, Dane, when Marcus screws up, we all pay the price. Like it or not, we have to find a way to deal with this. [*Dana seems to relent.*] Just try, ok? [*Dana wordlessly assents, and Deirdre goes over to comfort their mother. Dana watches them for a moment, then stalks out of the kitchen.*]

## ACT I

### Scene 2

[*A den filled with trophies and sports paraphernalia. Alvin Gaines sits on the edge of the sectional sofa, watching a basketball game. Dana stands in the doorway for a moment, fondly watching her father. Then she tries to brighten, and enters.*]

DANA: [*Knocks lightly on the doorframe.*] Hey, Daddy.

ALVIN: [*Stirs from his reverie and aims the remote at the big screen television. The game continues, but is muted.*] Dana? Dana! [*He rises with some difficulty, due to his bad knees and mild intoxication, and embraces his eldest daughter. She beams at him and they both sit back down on the sofa.*]

DANA: What you watching?

ALVIN: [*Embarrassed, he aims the remote and tries to turn off the television. Instead the game starts playing again, loudly. The sound flusters Alvin, who continues to shake the remote at the screen. We hear a sports announcer praising the athletic prowess of DeMarcus Gaines in a championship game. Finally, the screen goes dark and the room is quiet. Dana shifts uncomfortably on the couch and notices the bottle from which her father has been drinking. Alvin searches for something to say.*] I was just…cleaning up and I—I found some old tapes…[*Dana puts a hand on his shoulder.*]

DANA: You miss him, don't you?

ALVIN: I shouldn't, after what he's put this family through. But sometimes…I think about how things used to be. Your brother had such promise…

DANA: He owes all his success to you, Dad. You made Marcus into a teenage all-star.

ALVIN: [*Smiles, unable to hide his pride. He looks up at the wall, which is covered with markers of his son's success.*] I always hoped he'd turn out to be a "new and improved" version of his old man. Rookie of the year. Three championship rings.

DANA: Two-time MVP. And he isn't even thirty.

ALVIN: I don't know where I went wrong.

DANA: You can't blame yourself, Dad. Mom thinks the fame went to his head.

ALVIN: He was too young. We should have made him go to college—for two years, at least. Your brother was just so mature for his age—serious, thoughtful, not like other teenage boys. Your mother and I—we thought our kids were special.

DANA: And we were! How many black kids get to spend their childhood in Europe? You could have just retired back in '84, but you started a second career instead. You exposed us to different cultures, different languages. We were lucky to have a father like you.

ALVIN: But it didn't make you immune. We brought you back here and thought you wouldn't be susceptible to…[*Dana looks at him expectantly. Alvin struggles to explain himself.*] This country's sick, Dana. I can say that because I was born here, raised here. I made it to manhood despite America trying to trip me up with every kind of temptation. And now it's got my son by the throat… [*He reaches for his glass and takes a sip.*] …sooner or later they slip that noose around your neck, hoist you up, and leave you swinging in the breeze.

DANA: [*Measures her words.*] Marcus isn't being lynched, Dad.

ALVIN: That mob he's running from is out for blood!

DANA: The press wants the story—the full story, nothing more.

ALVIN: And the league? They'd like nothing better than to bury Marcus. His own teammates have turned against him, after he carried them on his back and turned that franchise around! And now the government's in on it, too—

DANA: Marcus can take care of that easily enough. All he has to do is turn his books over to the IRS. It might cost him an ounce of his pride and a few million dollars, but it's not going to cost him his life.

ALVIN: [*Sips his drink and grows bitter.*] Marcus was golden. They can't stand to see a black man shine.

DANA: You make it sound like it's some kind of conspiracy.

ALVIN: That's just what it is! One goddamn trap after another…

DANA: Marcus didn't have to take the bait, Dad. [*Alvin sits in sullen silence for a moment.*]

ALVIN: I tried to tell him—warn him what he'd be up against. The women, the reporters, the so-called friends always looking for a handout. But you can't coddle your son. He's got to stand on his own two feet. That's how a boy becomes a man.

DANA: Through trial and error?

ALVIN: I always hoped he'd learn from my mistakes. I tried to set a good example.

DANA: You did, Dad. You're the finest man I know.

ALVIN: [*Smiles and touches his daughter's face.*] It was so easy with you girls. You never gave us any trouble. [*His smile fades.*] What the hell happened to that boy? [*He drains his drink and nods to Dana to refill his glass. She hesitates, then reaches for the bottle on a nearby table and pours a little. Alvin insists she fill the glass, then settles back against the sofa, deep in thought.*] I never thought a son of mine would marry a white woman. [*He drains half the contents of his glass.*]

DANA: Mirlana isn't entirely white.

ALVIN: She sure as hell ain't black!

DANA: A lot of professional athletes are married to white women, Dad. It's a status symbol—you know that.

ALVIN: Hmph. "Trophy wife." A trophy is something you earn—something you take pride in. She's a goddamn stripper. [*He takes an angry swig at his drink.*]

DANA: Most trophies wind up collecting dust on a shelf. Mirlana is…ornamental.

ALVIN: She's Chinese?

DANA: [*Hides her smile and takes his drink away.*] Ornamental, Dad. She looks good on his arm.

ALVIN: The boy thinks with what's between his legs 'stead of what's between his ears.

DANA: Well, he didn't learn that from you. [*Alvin frowns.*]

ALVIN: I can't turn back time. I can't right his wrongs, or mine. But your brother won't get through this alone. We've got to help him, Dana.

DANA: You really think Marcus wants our help? It's been here all along.

ALVIN: I blame myself for that. I made him feel like he wasn't welcome, and that was wrong. A man shouldn't have to choose between his family and the woman he loves.

DANA: [*Soberly.*] No one should face that choice. But Marcus could have tried to meet you half way.

ALVIN: He's stubborn.

DANA: He's proud—too proud.

ALVIN: I never wanted my son to bow before anyone. I wanted him to walk upright, with his head held high.

DANA: There's a fine line between confidence and arrogance.

ALVIN: Yes, that's true. But it's a rare sight in this country, a black man with strong shoulders and a straight back. It felt good, seeing my boy stride across the court like a prince, looking like he owned everything beneath his feet.

DANA: And his swagger—the bling—the pimp attitude—how did that make you feel?

ALVIN: [*Pause.*] You know well as I do that a coach can't leave the bench. You run drills, you talk soft, sometimes—if you have to—you scream at your players. But once the game starts, they go out onto the court alone. And you just hope they remember what you taught 'em. Sometimes they run the play just like you called it. Sometimes they don't.

DANA: O'Leary said Marcus was "uncoachable."

ALVIN: O'Leary doesn't know his ass from his elbow.

DANA: [*Shrugs.*] He knows how to win championships.

ALVIN: That team would be nothing without Marcus.

DANA: They weren't that great with him. This season was their worst in years. They didn't even make the playoffs.

ALVIN: They were plagued by injuries, suspensions. Marcus was—distracted.

DANA: Team first, self second. Isn't that what you taught us?

ALVIN: [*Thankful for a chance to change the subject.*] Speaking of teams, how's yours?

DANA: Good. I think we've got a real shot at the championship this year.

ALVIN: You got a lot of young blood on that team. Rookies can be skittish.

DANA: I've got some veterans, too—or the closest thing to veterans in a league as young as ours.

ALVIN: You should be out there with them. You were a natural leader on the court. Led Team U.S.A. to Olympic gold!

DANA: My playing days are over, Dad. I don't want to end up with knees like yours.

ALVIN: [*Chuckles.*] Well, you had a good run. [*Dana nods, pleased.*] There wouldn't be a women's league if it weren't for players like you. When you stepped onto the court, there wasn't an empty seat in the entire stadium. You put women's college basketball on the map—even the networks sat up and took notice.

DANA: We didn't get half the media coverage—or half the money—that the men's programs got. But we certainly have come a long way.

ALVIN: You've given your whole life to the game.

DANA: Basketball's in my blood.

ALVIN: I always thought you'd be married by now, filling this house up with grandkids.

DANA: I've still got time.

ALVIN: [*Becoming drowsy.*] Don't wait too long—you'll have to take those fertility drugs, and God only knows what might happen. You could wind up with quintuplets—a whole team of Gaineses!

DANA: Now there's a scary thought.

ALVIN: What time is it? Shouldn't they be here by now?

DANA: I'll tell Deirdre to try Marcus' cell. Maybe their flight was delayed.

ALVIN: Maybe he changed his mind. Maybe that damn agent told him to stay away!

DANA: [*Stands.*] Relax, Dad. Why don't you go lie down for a little while? I'll come get you as soon as Marcus arrives. [*Alvin attempts to rise, then gives up and swings his legs up onto the sofa. He props a cushion under his head, and Dana drapes a throw over her father's long body. He closes his eyes immediately, and Dana watches him for a moment. Her gaze shifts to the walls, which are covered with framed pictures, newspaper articles, and awards. The room is like a shrine to DeMarcus. Only a small corner is reserved for her memorabilia. Disgusted, Dana turns and exits the den.*]

# ACT I

## Scene 3

[*The kitchen. Diane is still fussing over the food, while Deirdre sits at the table, holding her cell phone open in one hand. They are discussing Dana, but stop abruptly once Dana arrives.*]

DIERDRE: She's not fooling anyone.

DIANE: Well…you can't make her say it if she's not ready. [*Deirdre notices Dana approaching and signals to her mother to hush.*]

DEIRDRE: How's the old man?

DANA: Fast asleep.

DIANE: [*Annoyed.*] At this time of day? He was drinking, wasn't he? On an empty stomach, too.

DEIRDRE: We all got empty stomachs, Mom. When can we eat?

DIANE: As soon as your brother gets here. [*Diane sees Deirdre roll her eyes and so sets a plate of crudité on the table before her. Deirdre frowns but eats out of desperation and boredom.*]

DANA: I think Dad's nervous about Marcus coming…[*Sits at the breakfast bar.*] …with his not-quite-white wife. [*To Deirdre.*] Did you try his cell?

DEIRDRE: [*Nods and crunches into a carrot stick while looking at the screen of her cell phone.*] It went straight to voice mail. I'm texting him now.

DIANE: I hope everything's ok.

DEIRDRE: They probably just stopped to get a bite to eat.

DIANE: They better not! After I spent all day in this kitchen. [*Dana and Deirdre exchange worried glances. Deirdre indicates she isn't sure that everything is ok.*]

DANA: We are going to eat soon, right? I'm starving.

DIANE: [*Looks up at the clock, and then at the pots on the stove. She desperately wants Marcus to be the first to taste her feast, but now doubts he will arrive.*] Well, there's no point eating food that's overcooked…let's give him a few more minutes.

DEMARCUS: [*From offstage.*] Anybody home?

DIANE: He's here! [*Diane immediately springs into action, removing her apron, fixing her hair, rushing around the counter to be the first to greet her son. Dana and Deirdre exchange glances once more but remain seated. DeMarcus saunters into the kitchen, dressed in breezy casual attire. His platinum jewelry and diamond earring suggest opulence, though his demeanor is playful and easygoing. Mirlana enters behind him; she is diminutive, dressed in stylish, sexy clothes; she's anything but maternal. Her face is partly hidden by large tinted sunglasses and her long, straight hair.*] At last! We were starting to worry. [*She holds out her arms to embrace DeMarcus, who stoops to reach his mother.*]

DEMARCUS: Hey, Ma. Sorry we're late. Something came up. [*DeMarcus turns away from his mother before she can ask what. He spreads his arms out and stands before Deirdre, who rises on cue.*] Dee!

DEIRDRE: Hey, bro. Long time no see. [*DeMarcus wraps his arms around Deirdre, lifting her off the ground; she giggles like a child. Mirlana stands off to the side, watching them. Dana watches Mirlana, who is obviously uncomfortable despite her fixed smile. Hands clasped, Diane gazes adoringly at her son.*]

DEMARCUS: [*Deposits Deirdre and looks around the kitchen.*] Where my boys at?

DEIRDRE: [*Clears her throat, nervous.*] They're with their father this weekend.

DEMARCUS: [*Suddenly serious.*] Darnell?

DEIRDRE: [*Tries to reassure her brother.*] It's alright—his mom's visiting from St. Croix. [*DeMarcus nods, and searches Deirdre's eyes for signs of distress. Finding none, he turns to Dana who still hasn't risen from the breakfast bar.*]

DEMARCUS: [*His tone becomes playful again, but the embrace that follows lacks the warmth shown to Deirdre.*] And last but not least: Great Dane.

DANA: [*Tolerates the embrace, but barely adjusts her position on the stool.*] Hey, Marcus. Glad you could make it.

DEMARCUS: [*Ignores the implied criticism.*] It's about time we had a Gaines family reunion.

DANA: [*Dryly.*] Is that what you think this is?

DEMARCUS: [*Defiant.*] Sure. The gang's all here. [*He looks around the kitchen.*] Except for Pops.

DIANE: [*Hastily.*] Your father's sleeping. Deirdre, go wake him up! [*DeMarcus puts a hand on Deirdre's shoulder, keeping her in her seat.*]

DEMARCUS: That's alright, Dee. I got it. [*Before leaving the kitchen, he remembers Mirlana.*] Don't just stand there, girl. Come on in. They don't bite. [*He laughs and cuts his eyes at Dana. As DeMarcus exits, Diane rushes over to the stove.*]

DIANE: Marcus, don't you dare put that TV on. You just wake your father up and bring him straight to the dining room. I'll have this food on the table in less than five minutes—

DEMARCUS: Aw, that's alright, Ma. We grabbed something to eat on the road. [*He slaps the doorframe and exits, failing to see the disappointment in his mother's face. Dana stands, as if to go after him, but watches her mother instead.*]

DIANE: Oh, but—I… [*Diane stares into the steaming pots, and bites down on her lip to hold back tears. Mirlana seems embarrassed. Dana and Deirdre try to salvage the situation.*]

DEIRDRE: I don't know about you, ladies, but I say we forget the men and get our eat on! [*Goes over to her mother.*] What do you say, Mom? Leave the linen and the fancy china—let's just pile our plates and eat right here in the kitchen.

DIANE: [*Collects herself and smiles appreciatively at Dierdre.*] There's no point letting all this food go to waste!

DANA: That's right. Have a seat, Mirlana. You, too, Mom. We got this. [*Dana steers her mother over to the table and takes her place at the stove. Deirdre passes her a stack of plates; while Dana serves up the food, Deirdre takes out a bottle of wine and some wine glasses.*]

DIANE: Hello, dear. [*She and Mirlana smile and move towards one another for an awkward embrace.*] Please, have a seat. You must be tired from all that traveling.

MIRLANA: Actually, I was hoping I could lie down for a little while—

DIANE: [*Instantly maternal.*] Of course! Let me show you to your room.

DEIRDRE: [*Blocks them by coming around the counter with drinks.*] Girl, you have got to try our mother's gumbo. Here— [*Deirdre offers Mirlana a glass of wine, then remembers the miscarriage.*] Or— would you like something else to drink? Soda, or juice, or—

MIRLANA: [*Accepts the glass with another forced smile.*] No, this is fine. Thank you. [*Deirdre gestures for Mirlana to sit at the table. Next to the Gaines women, Mirlana looks like a child. She cowers before Deirdre and turns back toward the table.*]

DIANE: [*Pointedly.*] She's tired, Deirdre.

DANA: Maybe she just needs something hot to eat. [*Dana hands Deirdre a steaming plate, which she sets in front of Mirlana.*]

MIRLANA: [*Examines the food with interest and removes her purse from her shoulder.*] Well, I am a little hungry…we drove straight over from the airport. [*Dana pauses, realizing DeMarcus lied about eating on the road. Diane and Deirdre seem not to notice, and instead fuss over Mirlana, pulling out her chair, getting her cutlery, a napkin, etc. Dana continues to serve plates of steaming food, then comes around the counter and joins them at the table.*]

DIANE: Isn't this nice? Just us girls.

DANA: Mom, you really outdid yourself. This is a feast fit for a queen!

DIANE: [*Acts regal, and raises her glass for a toast.*] We're worth it.

DEIRDRE: [*Joins the toast, as do the others.*] Hell, yeah! [*There is an awkward silence, which the women fill by digging into their meal.*]

DIANE: So, Mirlana, how are my little granddaughters?

MIRLANA: [*Puts down her glass of wine and reaches for her tiny, expensive purse.*] I brought pictures. [*All three Gaines women respond with instant interest. Mirlana smiles with genuine warmth for *the first time, though she is still wearing the designer sunglasses. She hands the photos to Diane first, who then passes them along the table.*] This is Layla's first day at pre-school. That was taken at Christmas. And this is Easter. And this was taken at Lucelia's christening. [*She continues to hand the photos, one by one, to her in-laws until there are none left to share. To still her nervous hands, Mirlana reaches again for her wine glass.*]

DIANA: Oh, aren't they darling!

DEIRDRE: The littlest one—

MIRLANA: Lucelia.

DEIRDRE: Girl, she looks just like you! Right? [*She looks at Dana and Diane, who nod vigorously.*] Except she's got curly hair and yours is bone straight. I hope you don't mind, but is that your real hair? All of it, I mean. [*Stunned, Mirlana self-consciously touches her hair.*]

DANA: Dee!

DEIRDRE: What? I'm a professional, I'm allowed to ask. [*To Mirlana.*] I don't know if Marcus told you, but I own my own salon, and I get women in everyday asking for hair just like yours. You can buy it, of course, but Asian hair tends to be dark, and horse hair is easier to dye, but it can be brittle—

DANA: Enough, Deirdre.

DIANE: [*To Mirlana.*] Never mind her, dear. You have lovely hair.

MIRLANA: Thank you.

DIANE: [*Glares at Deirdre, then gathers the photos and hands them back to Mirlana.*] Thank you for bringing the photographs. I hope I'll get to meet my grandbabies someday soon.

MIRLANA: [*Accepts the photos and tucks them back in her purse.*] I wanted to invite you all to the christening, but Marcus said— [*Mirlana thinks better of sharing Marcus' words. Diane jumps in to fill the silence.*]

DIANE: Well, hopefully we can put all that unpleasantness behind us. I'm sure we don't have to tell you just how hard-headed the Gaines men can be.

DEIRDRE: They're probably up there butting heads right now.

DANA: I swear—we should just give them a ruler and tell them to get it over with already.

DIANE: Dana!

DANA: What? [*The three younger women smile. Diane shakes her head and takes a sip of wine, secretly pleased that the "reunion" is going so well. She keeps an eye on Dana, however, and so misses Deirdre's building aggression.*] So. Mirlana. What do you do? When you're not taking care of the girls, I mean.

MIRLANA: Well…sometimes I help organize fundraisers with the other wives.

DANA: [*Envisions Marcus with a harem.*] Other wives?

MIRLANA: The League Wives Association. We buy books for inner city schools, things like that.

DEIRDRE: That's great.

DIANE: I think it's wonderful that the players' wives have finally started their own organization. I wish I'd belonged to a group like that when I was your age. I had my children, of course, but when Al was on the road…it was kind of lonely sometimes. [*Mirlana nods sympathetically. Deirdre and Dana look at their mother, surprised by her revelation.*]

DEIRDRE: You never seemed lonely.

DANA: When I was little, you were always going to some meeting or event for your sorority.

DIANE: I left my sorors behind when we moved to Europe. I'm not saying my life lacked meaning. Just that being married to a professional athlete was like…being a pilot's wife, or being married to a military man. You're always praying they'll come home safe. Of course, with sports, an injury only ends your husband's career, not his life—though Al certainly acted like the stakes were just as high. [*She laughs.*] If your father's knees hadn't given out, I don't know if he'd have ever stopped playing. They practically had to drag him off the court!

DANA: I've tried to convince Dad to go into coaching. You know—high school or maybe college—work his way up to the NCAA. But he won't bite.

DIANE: He'd rather sit up there watching old highlight reels.

DANA: He'd rather start at the top—head coach of an NBA team.

DEIRDRE: [*To Mirlana.*] I'm sure we don't have to tell you just how big-headed the Gaines men can be.

MIRLANA: [*Quietly, nursing her drink.*] It's like a drug for them. [*She looks up and sees she has startled them.*] An addiction, I mean. When Marcus comes off the court after a win—he's so high, nothing can touch him.

DEIRDRE: Not even you and the girls?

MIRLANA: [*Her face darkens.*] Like your mom said, we don't get to see him that much.

DANA: Well, you'll be seeing a whole lot of him now that his team didn't make the playoffs.

MIRLANA: [*Self-consciously adjusts her sunglasses.*] Marcus isn't very good company these days. He doesn't like to lose. [*The Gaines women trade glances.*]

DEIRDRE: [*Defensively.*] Who does? Marcus is just under a lot of pressure right now. It's not easy being a superstar.

DANA: [*To Deirdre.*] And it's not easy being married to one. [*To Mirlana.*] I don't know how you've managed to smile through all the b.s.

MIRLANA: The paparazzi will do anything to catch you without a smile—those are the shots the tabloids really pay for. They don't want to see you happy. They want you to see you miserable and falling apart. [*Smoothes her hair again.*] I won't give them the satisfaction. [*An awkward pause.*]

DIANE: Players weren't treated like gods in my day.

DEIRDRE: They weren't demonized, either.

DANA: It's these multi-million dollar contracts. Players don't even focus on the game any more. They're too busy making rap albums and hanging out in strip clubs.

MIRLANA: Marcus might be in a movie.

DIANE: What?

MIRLANA: [*Nods eagerly.*] Monty got him an audition.

DEIRDRE: [*Excited.*] Oh yeah? Is it an action flick? I wonder who his co-star will be…[*Dana rolls her eyes.*] What? Shaq's made at least three movies.

DANA: And all of them were terrible! Marcus can't act.

DEIRDRE: [*Snide.*] Maybe you could give him some pointers, Dane.

MIRLANA: Monty's going to hire him an acting coach. If Marcus does well on his screen test, then he could go into film and television. Monty says it's important to think beyond the court.

DIANE: [*Disgusted.*] That man…

DEIRDRE: He's got a point, Mom. You said it yourself—one injury can end a player's career. Marcus needs to keep his options open.

MIRLANA: [*Timidly.*] Monty thinks I could start my own business.

DANA: [*Wary.*] Doing what?

DIANE: Not…dancing—

MIRLANA: [*Tilts her head, proud.*] Designing clothes. And accessories—handbags, shoes, jewelry. Maybe even perfume.

DEIRDRE: [*Sarcastic and bemused.*] Hey, why not? Look at J-Lo and Britney. If those bimbos can sell clothes—

DANA: Dee!

DEIRDRE: Sorry—that came out wrong. I just meant they don't have any real…training in fashion design.

MIRLANA: [*Defensive.*] Monty says it's more important to have a unique sense of style. I can hire designers to help me realize my vision. [*These last words are clearly not her own.*]

DIANE: Well. How exciting. I never knew you were so…ambitious.

DEIRDRE: Check the tattoo on her ass.

DANA: That's enough, Dee.

MIRLANA: [*Rises, in a huff.*] Where's Marcus?

DIANE: [*Stands and begins to clear the table.*] I don't know where he's gone off to. Why don't you girls go into the living room, and I'll make some coffee to have with dessert.

MIRLANA: [*Makes an effort to compose herself.*] I'd rather lie down now, Mrs. Gaines. Could you tell me which room I'll be staying in?

DEIRDRE: [*Stands and tries to use her height to once again intimidate Mirlana, but fails.*] You can't lie down now—you just ate. Come on—I promise I'll be nice…

MIRLANA: No, thank you. I'm tired—

DIANE: [*Tries to soothe Mirlana.*] Don't be angry, dear. I know it's awkward being here like this—

MIRLANA: [*Becomes hysterical and backs away from the other women.*] You hate me! I know you do—Marcus told me.

DIANE: That's not true!

MIRLANA: Yes, it is—you wouldn't even come to the wedding! It's been three years, and you haven't even seen our children! So I didn't go to college—so what! So I don't belong to a fancy sorority—and I never won a gold medal at the Olympics—and I don't own my own salon. So what! That doesn't make you better than me. [*She turns to storm out of the kitchen, then remembers her purse is on the table. She spins around, collides with Diane, then straightens herself and reaches for the bag. Deirdre grabs it first, and for a moment they fight over it.*]

DANA: [*Stands and pulls at her sister's arm.*] Deirdre, STOP! [*Deirdre lets go of the purse, and Mirlana falls back, knocking into Diane once more. The contents of her purse spill onto the kitchen floor. Mirlana hastily stoops to grab her belongings and as she stands up, loses her sunglasses.*]

DEIRDRE: [*Sees the black eye Mirlana has been trying to conceal.*] Oh, my God…

DANA: No—he—didn't…

DIANE: What? What's wrong? [*Mirlana scrambles for the sunglasses, but Deirdre reaches them first. Mirlana tries to use her long hair to shield her face. She turns away from the two sisters, but then must face Diane. Unable to look her mother-in-law in the eye, Mirlana starts to sob quietly. Diane gently pushes Mirlana's hair aside and examines the bruise around her right eye. When she finally speaks, Diane's voice is calm and deadly serious.*] Girls? Why don't you clean up in here. I'll take Mirlana up to her room. [*The sisters say nothing but do as they're told as Diane guides Mirlana out of the kitchen. Dana, clearly fuming, bangs the plates and pots as she clears up. Deirdre, stunned, moves slowly. Finally she sinks into an empty* chair. Dana slams a cupboard shut and stands at the sink, hands on hips.]

## ACT I

## Scene 4

[*A roiling hot tub on an outdoor deck. The sun is setting, and DeMarcus is laughing and drinking beer with Alvin.*]

ALVIN: [*Extends his arms and luxuriates in the steaming tub.*] Ahhh! The older I get, the better this feels.

DEMARCUS: You got to try the tub I got back in L.A., Dad. Custom made, eighteen jets, room for ten…[*They share a knowing glance and chuckle.*]…top of the line.

ALVIN: Only the best for my boy!

DEMARCUS: That's right! Matter of fact—why don't I get you an upgrade?

ALVIN: No!

DEMARCUS: Yeah! Soon as I get back, I'll call my guy and have him come out here and fix you up.

ALVIN: Your mother won't like it…

DEMARCUS: [*Makes a dismissive sound.*] Leave Ma to me.

ALVIN: [*Grows serious, but tries to keep it light.*] Your mother loves you, son.

DEMARCUS: [*Nods, sensing the tone has changed.*] I know.

ALVIN: It's been hard on her, not having you around. For your mother, living without you is like waking up each day without the sun up in the sky.

DEMARCUS: [*Defensive but respectful.*] I didn't ask to be disowned.

ALVIN: No, you didn't. And I'm sorry I let this...rift between us last as long as it has. [*He reaches for Marcus' shoulder.*] It's good to have you back, son.

DEMARCUS: [*Brightens and smiles at his father.*] It's good to be back.

ALVIN: I've done a lot of thinking these past few weeks, and I see now just how wrong I was to want you to do things my way. You're a man now, and you can't stand in my shoes any more than I can stand in yours. But I want you to know, son, you don't have to walk through life alone. We're here for you.

DEMARCUS: Thanks, Dad.

ALVIN: [*Waits for his son to make his own concession, but DeMarcus says nothing.*] So. I guess this season was kind of disappointing for you.

DEMARCUS: [*Makes a sound of disgust.*] Everybody says I need to share the ball more, but have you seen those rookies? When they're not turning the ball over, they're messing up plays, getting offensive fouls...it's a mess, Dad.

ALVIN: What's your coach got to say?

DEMARCUS: [*Sucks his teeth.*] O'Leary ain't the one calling the shots over there. You want change, you got to talk to the man in charge.

ALVIN: You went to the GM?

DEMARCUS: The owner! He asked me what I needed to win another championship, so I told him. And if I don't get it—I walk.

ALVIN: You'd consider a trade?

DEMARCUS: What choice do I have?

ALVIN: You got any particular team in mind?

DEMARCUS: I'm hoping it won't come to that.

ALVIN: You're bluffing?

DEMARCUS: I'm working with what I got. They want me, I want a starting line-up I can work with—<u>win</u> with. Monty's got his feelers out, and a few east coast teams are interested but...this is my home.

ALVIN: What happens if they call your bluff?

DEMARCUS: They won't.

ALVIN: You sure this Monty knows what he's doing?

DEMARCUS: After that trial, I thought my career was over. But Monty hired the best PR firm in the country. Sure, I lost a few key endorsements, but look at me now. Three years and I'm back on top of my game. Monty figures I'm worth close to half a billion dollars.

ALVIN: No wonder he's got you up on the auction block.

DEMARCUS: Dad—

ALVIN: You know your great-great-granddaddy was a slave. [*Marcus groans.*] I never talked about the past 'cause I didn't want you to think you owed anything to anyone. I'm a free man and so are you. You got where you are through your own blood, sweat, and tears.

DEMARCUS: That's right!

ALVIN: But white folks still see gold when they look at you, Marcus—black gold.

DEMARCUS: In this country—today—the only color that matters is green.

ALVIN: Don't think you're above history, son.

DEMARCUS: I'm not thinking about the past, Dad. I'm focused on the future.

ALVIN: That's all well and good, but I'm telling you, all that's passed ain't past. You found that out the hard way.

DEMARCUS: Aw, here we go…

ALVIN: You know what they used to do to a black man who dared to even look at a white woman?

DEMARCUS: I know what they tried to do to me!

ALVIN: That's nothing. You wrote a check and walked away clean—with all your body parts intact.

DEMARCUS: Don't worry, Dad, I learned my lesson.

ALVIN: [*Hopeful.*] You did?

DEMARCUS: Most definitely—next time I'll follow my teammates' advice: write the check <u>before</u> you sample the goods. [*Marcus chuckles but senses his father's disapproval.*] You know what it's like.

ALVIN: I know you got a wife, son.

DEMARCUS: You mean you never—

ALVIN: What? "Sampled the goods?" You think I'd do that to your mother? To you kids?

DEMARCUS: [*Resists the temptation to "out" his father.*] It's just sex, Dad! It's not love, it's not an affair—it's not even real. Like the guys say: you just hit it and quit it.

ALVIN: [*Pause.*] Did you rape that girl, Marcus?

DEMARCUS: What?!

ALVIN: You're sitting here talking like a pimp. You weren't raised to talk like that!

DEMARCUS: Like I told the cops—I thought it was consensual…

ALVIN: Did you even bother to ask?

DEMARCUS: Man, I don't have to ask! Those 'hos are giving it away.

ALVIN: And you just take it without thinking twice about your family, your reputation, your health—how you going to look your wife in the eye and tell her you gave her a disease?

DEMARCUS: Today's playas don't worry about that.

ALVIN: Really. You think you're bigger than AIDS?

DEMARCUS: You seen Magic lately? It's a brand new game, Dad. Different players, different rules.

ALVIN: [*Takes a moment to control his emotion and tries a different approach.*] What happened to the rules we taught you, son?

DEMARCUS: [*Sarcastic.*] What—like the Ten Commandments?

ALVIN: Maybe we should have raised you in the church.

DEMARCUS: [*Mockingly, like a "holy roller."*] Jesus saves!

ALVIN: [*Sadly.*] Is there anything you fear, son?

DEMARCUS: You want me to be afraid?

ALVIN: I want you to respect your own limits. You can't do everything, Marcus.

DEMARCUS: Why not? Ever since I was a little kid, you told me I could do anything—be anything I wanted to be. What's changed?

ALVIN: You've changed. You're becoming someone we don't even recognize anymore.

DEMARCUS: Oh—so I'm a stranger now?

ALVIN: That's not what I said.

DEMARCUS: Family's supposed to stand by you through thick and thin. But soon as the shit hit the fan—where were you? Nowhere to be found!

ALVIN: You made a choice, Marcus. You listened to your boys, you listened to Monty—you listened to everyone but me!

DEMARCUS: You're not my coach anymore, Dad! And you're not my manager. You're my <u>father</u>—you're supposed to stand by me no matter what!

ALVIN: I am your father, and I love you more than you'll ever know, son. Your mother and I—your sisters, too—we love you unconditionally. But this isn't about love, Marcus. It's about right and wrong.

DEMARCUS: And you're going to lecture me about ethics? [*He adopts a menacing tone.*] You sure that's something you want to do, Dad?

ALVIN: [*Retreats and grows quiet.*] I don't want to fight you, Marcus. I'm not your enemy. I asked you here this weekend so we could find a way to work together—

DEMARCUS: [*Sarcastic.*] Like a team?

ALVIN: Like a family. This situation you've gotten yourself into—it's serious! And not even Monty the magician can make it disappear. We want to help you, son. Are you willing to work with us?

DEMARCUS: [*Pause. Marcus gauges the potential cost of cooperating.*] So long as you treat me like a man. I'm not a kid anymore, Dad-

DIANE: Boy! [*Diane storms out onto the deck, catching Alvin and DeMarcus by surprise.*]

DEMARCUS: Hey, Ma. What's up?

DIANE: You!

DEMARCUS: What?

DIANE: Get up! [*She grabs a towel and hurls it at him.*]

DEMARCUS: [*The towel hits him in the face.*] Ma!

ALVIN: Woman, what's wrong with you?

DIANE: You get out that tub right now, DeMarcus Gaines, or I'll come in there and haul you out myself! [*DeMarcus looks at his father who is just as amazed. Marcus slowly rises from the tub but sits on its edge rather than emerging fully. He pats himself dry and puts the towel around his shoulders to keep warm. Diane begins pacing the deck.*] All this time…all this time I defended you!

ALVIN: Di, please. Will you just tell us what's going on?

DIANE: Sure, Al. I'll tell you what's going on. Your son's wife is inside crying herself to sleep.

ALVIN: What? [*To Marcus.*] Why?

DEMARCUS: [*Shrugs.*] She was fine when I left her. Maybe the Great Dane went on the attack.

DIANE: Don't you dare blame your sister for this!

ALVIN: [*Frustrated.*] For what?

DIANE: [*To Marcus.*] Are you going to tell him, or am I?

DEMARCUS: [*Nonchalant.*] That's why you're out here, right?

DIANE: You got a lot of nerve talking to me like that, boy. [*To Alvin.*] Your daughter-in-law's got a black eye.

ALVIN: What!?

DEMARCUS: It was an accident—we were fooling around and—

DIANE: What? She fell into your fist? [*Alvin gets out of the hot tub and puts on a terry robe. He wants to align himself with Diane, but she is still pacing and rejects Al's attempts to still her.*] All this time…all this time I kept saying, "Not my boy! Not MY son!" All this time I believed in you. I defended you!

[*Marcus turns his head away, but it is unclear whether he is ashamed or annoyed.*]

ALVIN: Di—give the boy a chance to explain himself.

DIANE: [*Spins around and points at Alvin.*] YOU stay out of this! It's your bad example he's been following!

ALVIN: [*Outraged.*] Me? I never raised my hand against you!

DIANE: You never hit me, but you hurt me in other ways, Al. We never talk about it, and I never told the girls, but that doesn't mean my heart isn't still bleeding after all these years. Look at him. [*Al hangs his head, but Diane lunges at him, commanding his attention.*] LOOK AT HIM! Did you tell your son not to cheat on his wife, or did you tell him <u>not</u> to get caught? [*Al looks at Marcus, but his son refuses to make eye contact. Diane spins around to face Marcus once more.*] Boy, I'm a tell you one more time—GET OUT OF THAT DAMN TUB! [*Without looking at either of his parents, Marcus gets out of the hot tub and begins drying off.*] You go to your wife and you apologize, you hear me?

DEMARCUS: [*Sullen.*] I already did…

DIANE: [*Moves toward Marcus, her voice and demeanor menacing. But Diane won't allow herself to get too close for fear of striking him.*] Don't you talk back to me. You take your behind inside that house and say it like you mean it! And if you can't do that—if you can't promise your wife it won't EVER happen again—then you take yourself right on out of my house. And don't bother coming back. [*Marcus pulls on some shorts and heads inside without looking at either of his parents. Diane, still fuming, tries to calm herself. Al stands awkwardly behind her, wanting to say or do something. He reaches for Diane but she seems to sense it and begins pacing again.*] I didn't raise a brute. He doesn't get this from me!

ALVIN: Di—

DIANE: Is it in your DNA? Is that it? Or is it some kind of virus you all pick up in the locker room?

ALVIN: [*Helplessly.*] We're human, Di.

DIANE: [*Spins to face him.*] So am I, Alvin! So is our daughter-in-law. [*Pause.*] And so was the girl in that hotel.

ALVIN: Hold on, now, Diane. You and I both know our son didn't rape that girl. He was in the wrong place at the wrong time—

DIANE: [*Clamps her hands over her ears.*] STOP! Just stop it, Al! [*She softens and pleads with him.*] Stop making excuses for him. [*Diane weakens suddenly and sinks onto a bench on the deck.*] I don't know where we went wrong. But we can't prop him up any more. [*Long pause.*]

ALVIN: So what do we do now?

DIANE: I don't know, Al. I don't know.

[*Alvin gauges her emotion and decides it's now safe to approach. He slowly crosses the deck and tries to put a hand on her shoulder. Diane flinches and pulls away. Al accepts her rejection, and sits down on the bench, leaving space between them. They sit in silence, pondering the fate of their troubled son.*]

# ACT I

## Scene 5

[*The kitchen, 3am. Dana wanders in wearing her pajamas. She looks somewhat disheveled, but angry and alert. Deirdre is seated at the table wearing a plain cotton robe over her nightgown. Her eyes are bleary, either from drinking, crying, or lack of sleep.*]

DEIRDRE: [*Softly.*] Some family reunion, huh?

DANA: [*Looks at her sister and softens somewhat. She goes over to the counter and fills the electric kettle with water.*] Tea? [*Deirdre nods, but continues to stare at the table top. Dana watches her as she gets out two mugs, the teabags, etc.*] Couldn't sleep?

DEIRDRE: [*Pause.*] Did you hear Mom screaming at Marcus?

DANA: She wasn't screaming, Dee.

DEIRDRE: I've never seen her that angry before.

DANA: She's never seen her son in that light before.

DEIRDRE: You think it's true then.

DANA: [*Freezes, and tries to contain her emotion.*] True? You saw her, Dee. You think she faked a black eye?

DEIRDRE: [*Almost mumbles.*] She must have done something...

DANA: [*Furious but controlled.*] She had it coming—is that it? She asked to be punched in the face?

DEIRDRE: I'm just saying, there are two sides to every story.

DANA: And what did Marcus have to say for himself? [*Deirdre makes no reply and the kettle begins to boil. Dana turns away from her sister and makes the tea. She brings the mugs over, sets one before Deirdre, and then sits at the far end of the table. As she waits for her tea to cool, Dana's anger dissipates and she becomes contemplative.*] Remember when it was just us?

DEIRDRE: Us who?

DANA: You and me. Before Marcus was born.

DEIRDRE: That was a long time ago, Dane. We were little kids then—not much older than Marcus' girls.

DANA: I remember those days.

DEIRDRE: [*Pause.*] You wish he'd never been born, don't you.

DANA: I wish I never found out what it feels like to be second best.

DEIRDRE: You know, when I was a kid, I used to pray God would make me athletic so I'd fit in around here. But now I'm glad I never learned to dribble a damn ball. Why does everything between you and Marcus have to be a competition? Why can't you just be you, Dana?

DANA: Because who I am isn't good enough. Not for them. [*Deirdre frowns.*] And don't tell me it's all in my head.

DEIRDRE: You've been playing that tape for a real long time, Dane.

DANA: What tape?

DEIRDRE: [*In an automated voice.*] It goes a little something like this: life was bliss until Marcus was born; that evil boy stole my birthright. Stop. Rewind. Play. Life was bliss until Marcus was born...

DANA: God. You always take his side.

DEIRDRE: Whatever happened to all of us being on the same team?

DANA: There's no "I" in team, Deirdre. Marcus has never thought of anyone but himself.

DEIRDRE: He's a good father. You could tell just from those pictures how much he loves his daughters.

DANA: I'll bet he doesn't love them like he loves his son.

DEIRDRE: [*Is reluctant to engage her sister on this point, but must respond somehow.*] We don't know that that's his kid. Women are always trying to trap famous men that way.

DANA: If it's not his, why didn't Marcus ask for a paternity test? Why is he paying her child support?

DEIRDRE: At least give him credit for acknowledging the boy. Men walk away from their kids every day. Look at Darnell!

DANA: Is that what you do, Dee? Compare Marcus to Darnell? No wonder he never loses his shine!

DEIRDRE: He's our brother, Dana. It's called loyalty.

DANA: [*Slams her hand on the table.*] Loyalty is earned! He's done nothing to deserve our support.

DEIRDRE: He doesn't have to—it's supposed to be automatic!

DANA: It's not like that for everyone.

DEIRDRE: You can say what you want about Marcus, but at least he's not trying to be something he's not. Marcus is legit.

DANA: Legit? He's a bona fide rapist—is that what you mean?

DEIRDRE: Those charges were dropped!

DANA: Sure they were—Johnny Cochrane worked yet another miracle for yet another rich client! But Johnny's dead now, Dee. What's Marcus going to do the next time he's arrested? Which could be any day now...

DEIRDRE: I don't know, Dane—maybe you could show him how to keep up appearances.

DANA: [*Confused.*] What are you talking about? You know damn well Marcus won't take advice from me.

DEIRDRE: Have you ever wondered why?

DANA: No, Dee. I don't have to wonder—I know he's an arrogant, ignorant, chauvinist pig! He doesn't listen to any woman whose I.Q. is higher than his shoe size.

DEIRDRE: So I'm dumb.

DANA: That's not what I meant. You've always been Marcus's... cheerleader. [*Deirdre mockingly hoists her pompoms.*] You're like Mom, Dee. You cook for him, clean up after him. Stroke his ego whenever it's bruised.

DEIRDRE: Marcus respects me because I'm honest, Dane. I tell him just what I think and why.

DANA: Marcus respects your opinion because it matches his own. [*Deirdre looks angry, then hurt.*] What?

DEIRDRE: Don't you trust me, Dane? [*Dana frowns. Deirdre sucks up her courage and speaks deliberately.*] I think it's time for you to come clean.

DANA: What are you talking about?

DEIRDRE: Come out, Dana. [*Dana's mouth falls open for a moment, but she quickly gathers herself and remains in control. She admits and denies nothing.*] Marcus blows you off because he thinks you're a fraud.

DANA: I don't give a shit what he thinks...

DEIRDRE: Yes, you do. I know you do.

DANA: No, Dee. YOU do. I swear to God, ever since you left Darnell...

DEIRDRE: Don't go there, Dane.

DANA: Why not? Aren't you the one lecturing me on the importance of being honest?

DEIRDRE: There are things you don't know about me and Darnell.

DANA: Like what? That he knocked the sound out your left ear?

DEIRDRE: [*Flashes her eyes at Dana and then looks away, angry but also ashamed.*] You knew.

DANA: We all knew. In fact, we had a good old-fashioned family conference call to figure out what to do.

DEIRDRE: You didn't have to do anything. Marcus took care of it. He took care of me.

DANA: By paying some thugs to rough Darnell up? You're grateful to Marcus for that? At least Dad was willing to kick Darnell's ass himself.

DEIRDRE: Thanks to Marcus, that wasn't necessary.

DANA: [*With contempt.*] So he's your savior.

DEIRDRE: He's our brother. Our baby brother!

DANA: Marcus is a grown man, Dee.

DEIRDRE: And you're a grown woman. Why should Marcus act with integrity when you don't? [*Dana fights the urge to spit out a reply. Instead she screws up her lips and turns away. Deirdre regrets her tone, but decides she's gone too far to turn back.*] How's Lynn?

DANA: [*Long pause. Then quietly, but with pride.*] She's pregnant.

DEIRDRE: [*Stunned, she reaches for her sister.*] Oh, my God! Dana, that's wonderful! I didn't even know you two were trying...

DANA: Well, like you said, Dee—I'm a master of deception.

DEIRDRE: [*Pulls back, shamed.*] You could've told me, Dane. You know I'd never judge you...

DANA: [*Laughs ironically.*] Oh, please! You looked that girl in the face—you SAW her black eye, and you STILL think Marcus is innocent. And when I object, you call me a traitor. I should trust YOU? [*Deirdre opens her mouth but can think of nothing to say. Dana builds up steam and goes on.*] Darnell knocked you around—in front of your kids, he knocked you around. But when you look at Marcus, you only see what you want to see. That's what I'm up against, Deirdre. That's what my child will be up against. And you wonder why I don't advertise my relationship with Lynn?

DEIRDRE: It's a new day, Dana. For God's sake, the vice-president's daughter is gay!

DANA: Dick Cheney's got nothing on Mom and Dad.

DEIRDRE: You don't have to hide how you feel. Everybody knows, anyway.

DANA: If everybody knows, then why do I have to make a formal announcement? I'm entitled to my privacy.

DEIRDRE: We just want you to be proud of who you are.

DANA: [*Sits back, not ready to be patronized.*] You think I'm ashamed of being gay? That's what you think?

DEIRDRE: Why else would you keep Lynn a secret?

DANA: Because my love life is MY business, Dee! I choose not to live in the tabloids.

DEIRDRE: No offense, Dane, but it's really not that deep. Enquiring minds don't want to know what you do in your bedroom. Besides, everyone knows that half the players in your league are gay.

DANA: Really. And just how does "everyone" know that?

DEIRDRE: [*Sheepishly.*] Words gets around…

DANA: People talk, you mean. I'll bet your customers just love to speculate. They look at us—at a woman like me—and say, "Damn, she's big as a man! An Amazon! And look at her hair! I bet she's funny." That's what the "sistas" say when they sit down in your chair for a press and curl, right?

DEIRDRE: Look—I know there are lipstick lesbians, but you got to admit, Dane—some of those girls you play with are <u>rough</u>!

DANA: What's wrong with women being strong, or aggressive, or even dominant? Men act that way on and off the court, and they're fucking worshipped. Women act that way and we're called "nappy-headed 'hos." It's such bullshit!

DEIRDRE: [*Discreetly primps her hair.*] If you ask me, sisters were more upset about being called nappy-headed than they were about being called 'hos. And while we're on the subject, you should let me tighten up those locks…

DANA: Are you listening to me, Dee?

DEIRDRE: Of course, I am! I've been wanting us to have this conversation for years.

DANA: Why?

DEIRDRE: I wanted you to know that it's ok to be…you!

DANA: You think I'm a bitter, self-hating lesbian, and so you wanted me to bare my soul, unburden myself to you.

DEIRDRE: It can't be easy living in the closet.

DANA: [*Laughs mockingly.*] Oh, God, Dee—you watch too much TV.

DEIRDRE: I have gay friends, you know—I am a hairstylist! I know all about the scene—

DANA: The scene?

DEIRDRE: You know—the underground network of…women who like women.

DANA: You can't even say the word out loud. I'm a LESBIAN, Dee. What would happen if I came by your salon? Better yet—what do you tell people about me when I'm not around?

DEIRDRE: What do you mean? Everybody knows I have a big sister who plays ball. Just like everybody knows I have a little brother who plays ball.

DANA: Well, the whole damn world knows how much Marcus likes women. What do they know about me?

DEIRDRE: [*Hedges.*] They know you're an athlete.

DANA: And?

DEIRDRE: And…sometimes folks ask me why you're not married.

DANA: [*Smiles, enjoying Dee's discomfort.*] And what do you tell them, Dee?

DEIRDRE: That you don't have time for men. That you're used to being the one who calls the shots, and brothers just aren't having it. I don't lie. I omit the truth—just like you.

DANA: I'm not ashamed of who I am, Dee.

DEIRDRE: Then why not tell Mom and Dad?

DANA: You just said "everybody knows." Seems to me the policy in this family is, "Don't ask, don't tell." If they want to hear me say it, they can ask. I won't lie.

DEIRDRE: But that's so wrong! Not talking about it makes it seem like it's something dirty.

DANA: And talking about it will make it clean? I don't need anybody quoting the bible at me.

DEIRDRE: Please! Who in this family COULD quote the bible? Mom just wants you to be happy.

DANA: She thinks I hate Marcus because I'm a lesbian. You think that too, don't you?

DEIRDRE: [*Pause.*] You are pretty hard on him, Dane.

DANA: [*Shakes her head, disgusted and frustrated.*] You see? This is why I can't just "be me." Because everything I say gets read the wrong way. I locked my hair because I'm a lesbian. I coach women's basketball because I'm a lesbian. I don't support my no-count brother because I'm a lesbian. Everything—the way I dress, the way I talk—all of it gets reduced to this. To one small piece of my identity.

DEIRDRE: Small? It seems pretty major to me. I mean, you basically gave up on men.

DANA: [*Sighs, annoyed.*] Let me break it down for you, Dee. Straight women give up on men. They have this "happily ever after" fantasy that inevitably falls apart. I never had that fantasy, Dee. I didn't <u>give up</u> on men—I just don't want to <u>get up</u> on men.

DEIRDRE: Still, you seem kind of hostile sometimes.

DANA: Towards Marcus, yes. But I'm not like that with Dad, or any other man who acts like a decent human being. Every woman has the right to reject any man who disrespects her. You rejected Darnell! Do you support Marcus because you're straight? You've been in an abusive relationship yet you side with him over Mirlana. Is that because you just LOVE men?

DEIRDRE: No! My sexual preference has nothing to do with it.

DANA: Neither does mine. But anytime <u>I</u> step out of line—anytime *I* dare to challenge the status quo, sex gets thrown in my face. I'm wrong because I'm not ladylike, not feminine enough. I don't go weak in the knees every time I see a picture of Denzel. Ergo, I'm unnatural.

DEIRDRE: I don't think that way, Dane.

DANA: Yes, you do. Otherwise I'd have come out to you a long time ago, Dee. [*There is a long pause. Deirdre is deeply hurt and Dana is sorry for causing her pain. She tries to make amends by sharing details of her relationship.*] I met Lynn when I first got drafted into the league. She was assistant coach in Memphis, and then after a year, I got traded to Houston. We both felt an attraction during that year, but we never acted on it. We kept it strictly professional—for our own sake, and for the league.

DEIRDRE: Why would the league care? People fall in love on the job all the time.

DANA: If a man and a woman fall in love, people say, "Nature ran its course." It's not like that for us, Dee. The league is supposed to be all about empowering women, but if people start to think of us as "just a bunch of lesbians," then we risk losing our target audience, our corporate sponsors—it would be over before it even began.

DEIRDRE: [*Sobered.*] So when did you and Lynn…hook up?

DANA: We kept in touch while I was in Texas. She took a job on the west coast, and when I retired as a player, I moved out there too. The rest is history.

DEIRDRE: Uh—you left out a few chapters, Dane. What about the baby?

DANA: We figured since I was younger, it would be best for me to get pregnant. I took all kinds of injections, hormones, vitamins—I felt like a lab rat. But we were so excited about starting a family…we kept trying and trying, but the in vitro procedure just didn't work. [*Quietly.*] I had three miscarriages.

DEIRDRE: Dana!

DANA: So finally we decided to try Lynn's womb instead. She's over forty, but so far the baby's doing just fine.

DEIRDRE: How far along is she?

DANA: We just passed the three-month mark. The baby's due around Thanksgiving. [*Pause. With some satisfaction.*] It's a boy. [*She waits to see Deirdre's eyebrows go up.*] But don't worry—I promise not to castrate the little tyke at birth.

DEIRDRE: [*Blushes, fearing Dana read her thoughts.*] And the father?

DANA: Anonymous donor. [*She anticipates Dee's next question.*] He's black.

DEIRDRE: [*Nods wordlessly.*] You'll be a great mom, Dana. I'm sorry I— [*Deirdre searches for the right words.*] I'm sorry I wasn't the sister you needed.

DANA: It's ok. I've always known where your loyalty lies.

DEIRDRE: I still think there's good inside of him, Dane. He's not a monster! Marcus is worth saving.

DANA: Marcus doesn't want to BE saved, Dee. He doesn't want to BE the damsel in distress. He wants to be the knight on the white horse, charging in to save the day. That's the only role he's willing to play.

DEIRDRE: He still needs us.

DANA: When it comes out of his mouth, then I'll know. [*She examines the dregs at the bottom of her cup, then rises and takes it over to the sink.*] What time are we meeting tomorrow?

DEIRDRE: I think Dad said 9am.

DANA: Better get some sleep, then. [*Dana waits for Deirdre to rise, but she remains seated at the table.*] I'm going up.

DEIRDRE: [*Rouses herself from reverie, but doesn't rise.*] Goodnight, Dane.

DANA: Goodnight, Dee. [*Dana exits, leaving Deirdre alone in the kitchen.*]

## ACT I

## Scene 6

[*Deirdre walks down the dimly lit hall, stopping in front of the guest room where DeMarcus and Mirlana are staying. She raises her hand to knock, then hesitates and puts her ear up to the door. We hear the sounds of sex, Mirlana climaxing. Deirdre hovers for a moment, then she continues down the hall and enters her own room.*]

## ACT II

## Scene 1

[*The living room. The entire Gaines family is gathered to discuss DeMarcus' current crisis. Alvin stands near the center of the room, leaning against the fireplace mantle. DeMarcus and Mirlana, hands clasped, sit in a loveseat on one side of the room. Dana and Deirdre sit facing them on another sofa. Diane sits regally in a wing back chair, close to where Alvin is standing.*]

ALVIN: Alright, let's get down to business. I called this meeting because of the current…crisis facing our family.

DANA: Facing Marcus, you mean.

ALVIN: What happens to your brother affects us all, Dana. And it will take all of us working together to make this right. Now, son, why don't you begin by telling us your side of the story.

DEMARCUS: [*Sullen.*] What do you want to know?

DIANE: [*Stern.*] The truth.

DANA: The whole truth.

DEMARCUS: "And nothing but." You want me to swear on a bible or something?

DEIRDRE: [*Looks at him meaningfully so he knows she's on his side.*] You're not on trial, Marcus. But you know what they're saying about you in the media. Somebody shot up that club, and somebody's going to have to pay for it. We just need to know what's true—and we need to hear it from you.

DIANE: I just don't understand how you manage to keep getting yourself mixed up in these…scandals!

ALVIN: That's why we're here, Di. Seems to me, son, you've got some explaining to do.

DEMARCUS: [*Releases his wife's hand and leans forward.*] First of all, I haven't been charged with anything.

DANA: Yet.

DIANE: The papers say you're under investigation…

DEIRDRE: He's a person of interest, Mom, not a suspect.

DANA: What's the difference?

DEMARCUS: The difference is, I didn't do it!

DANA: Then who did?

[*Marcus looks smug and leans back again.*]

ALVIN: If you lie down with dogs, son, you're going to wake up with fleas. When did you start running with these—these—?

DIANE: Thugs! They're just using you, Marcus, can't you see that?

DEMARCUS: Those "thugs" are my friends.

ALVIN: You never used to have friends like that!

DEMARCUS: I never used to have friends at all, Dad. Remember? I had basketball.

DEIRDRE: And us. You always had us.

DEMARCUS: Maybe that was true…[*He looks away.*] …back in the day.

ALVIN: Speak your mind, son.

DEMARCUS: [*Hesitates, then lifts his chin and proceeds.*] They say blood is thicker than water, but where've you been these past few years? You don't like the people I hang with, well at least they know something about loyalty. [*He puts an arm around Mirlana and she flushes with pride.*]

DANA: Oh, yeah? You think they're going to stand by you when you get sent to prison?

DIANE: Your grandmother used to say, "Show me your friends and I'll tell you who you are."

ALVIN: Just what have these "friends" done for you?

DEMARCUS: They're useful for…certain things.

DIANE: Like what?

DEMARCUS: [*Looks straight at Deirdre, who looks away.*] Protection. A man in my position has to be careful when he goes out into the world. [*He glares at Dana.*] Everybody's trying to bring a brother down.

ALVIN: So why not hire professional bodyguards? This…entourage brings nothing but drama to your life. You get into trouble trying to protect them on the court, and then they get you into trouble everywhere else!

DEMARCUS: Come on, Dad—what would you do if some punk sucker-punched your teammate? Sit on the bench and do nothing? [*Alvin looks away. Dana, disappointed in her father, jumps in.*]

DANA: You let the referees handle it. You don't start a brawl with the entire opposing team. And you definitely don't take a swing at a fan!

MIRLANA: They were throwing things at them—beer, even chairs! I was there. They had to defend themselves.

DIANE: It was disgraceful! You all acted like a bunch of high school hooligans.

ALVIN: Those suspensions cost you the series, son.

DEMARCUS: Yeah, well—that's how we roll. "All for one…"

DANA: "…and one for all." Is that why you were at that strip joint? Thought you'd treat your boys to a little post-game entertainment?

[*Mirlana flinches but smoothes her hair to compose herself.*]

DEMARCUS: Sure. Nothing wrong with having a little fun at a gentleman's club. You should come with us some time, Dane. I bet you'd like it.

DIANE: Stop it! How dare you sit there and talk about this—filth! In front of your wife! [*Marcus looks at the floor. Mirlana glances at him then speaks to Diane.*]

MIRLANA: Marcus promised he'd never go back—

DANA: He promised to love, honor, and cherish you, too. How's that working out?

DEIRDRE: Can we get back to the real issue here? Marcus, what does your attorney say?

DEMARCUS: That I got nothing to worry about. It wasn't my gun fired those shots.

DIANE: [*Shocked.*] Since when do you carry a gun?

DEMARCUS: Since one of my teammates got robbed at home—<u>those</u> thugs tied him and his family up, put duct tape over their mouths, and then stripped the place clean.

DIANE: Oh, my God!

DANA: So if your gun didn't go off, whose did?

[*Marcus ignores his sister's question. Alvin persists.*]

ALVIN: Well?

DEMARCUS: I look like a snitch to you?

ALVIN: [*Charges at his son, shaking with rage.*] Boy, you better quit acting like some kind of ghetto thug! You weren't raised in the street! You've had advantages most of your teammates only dream about, and yet you've brought nothing but shame on this family.

DEIRDRE: Dad—

ALVIN: No—I'm through coddling you. You want to be treated like a man, then stop posing and start acting like one! If you're so proud of your "friends" and the life you all live, then stand up and admit what you've done! I've had enough of your secrets.

DEMARCUS: [*Becomes menacing.*] I'm not the only one with secrets, am I? [*Dana braces herself, but Marcus' gaze is fixed on his father.*] A real man tells the truth—right, Dad? And if he makes a mistake, a real man stands up and faces the consequences. Right, Dad? [*Alvin tries to meet his son's gaze but finally yields before Marcus' implied threat.*]

DIANE: [*Watches her son with a mixture of disgust and fear. She glances up at Alvin, then turns to face Deirdre and Dana.*] Girls, there's something I never told you about…about my relationship with your father

DEMARCUS: Ma—you don't have to—

DIANE: [*Ignores him and goes on.*] I swore I'd never tell you this—I wanted to protect you, and…I suppose there was a part of me that was ashamed.

DANA: Ashamed? Of what?

DIANE: [*Reaches for and clasps Alvin's hand. He turns to face the mantle.*] It wasn't always easy, being married to an athlete. There were times when—your father I were apart more than we were together.

DEIRDRE: [*Nods, recalling yesterday's conversation.*] You were like a pilot's wife.

DIANE: That's right.

DANA: Oh, God... [*Dana closes her eyes and steels herself. Alvin tries to move farther away but Diane holds fast to his hand.*]

DIANE: [*Focuses on Deirdre, who has assumed the demeanor of a little girl.*] All couples have...difficulties. You know that, Dee. Sometimes the marriage can't be saved. But sometimes, if two people truly love one another, and they're willing to work, they can repair the damage and move on.

DEIRDRE: [*Unable to accept the obvious truth.*] You...had an affair?

ALVIN: [*Finally turns to face his daughters.*] No, Dee. I did.

DEIRDRE: Dad!

DIANE: I promised your father I wouldn't tell you girls, and we got beyond the affair—we became closer, even. That was around the time your brother was conceived...

DANA: You didn't tell us about this affair, but you told Marcus?

DIANE: I thought—if he knew how much it hurts a woman—how close your father and I came to losing each other...it might help him be a better husband to his own wife. [*She spins to face Marcus.*] I never dreamed he'd use it against your father this way. Boy, I swear, sometimes I don't know who you are.

DEMARCUS: [*Jumps up, irate.*] You all keep saying that, but what makes me so different from any of you? You all got secrets! And you—[*He points at Dana.*] You're the biggest hypocrite of all!

DEIRDRE: Marcus, don't! [*Dee moves to leap up but Dana grabs her and holds her down.*]

DANA: Let him talk, Dee.

DEMARCUS: That's right, and you all might as well get comfortable 'cause I got plenty to say.

DANA: [*Folds her arms across her chest, defiant.*] Let's hear it then.

DEMARCUS: You walk around here like you're some kind of saint, but we all know what kind of sinner you are.

DIANE: Leave your sister alone, Marcus. This isn't about her—

DEMARCUS: No—as always, it's all about me. It's my lifestyle and my friends that's the problem. But what about her, huh? What do you all think about Dana's special friend?

DEIRDRE: [*Breaks Dana's grasp and stands to confront her brother.*] I'm warning you, Marcus—leave her alone!

DEMARCUS: [*Stares her down.*] Or what, Dee? We both know you can't put up much of a fight. [*Deirdre reels as if struck. Marcus regrets his words, but cannot stop himself.*] You're supposed to be on MY side, Dee! I was there when you needed me.

DEIRDRE: No, you weren't! You sent your boys to do your dirty work for you.

DEMARCUS: I told you I'd handle it, and I did.

DEIRDRE: That's right, little brother. Thanks to you, Darnell's gone. But look how you "handle" your wife!

DEMARCUS: Here we go again! Why is everybody always pointing the finger at ME? You all see how Dana treats me—you know she's always been jealous of me! [*He pushes past Deirdre to face Dana, who remains calmly seated.*] I'm sick of your holier-than-thou bullshit, Dana! You think you got everybody fooled, but not me. I know what you are. And I know why you're always hatin' on me. You want what I got—right? The money, the fame, the championship rings. I bet you even got your eye on my wife… [*Under his breath but audible to all.*] Dyke! [*Diane bursts forth and tries to slap Marcus across the face. He pulls back and tries to restrain her, but Diane continues to pound at him. Alvin and Deirdre try to pull them apart. In the midst of the melee, the doorbell rings. Everyone freezes for a moment. Mirlana, looking terrified, moves towards the door.*]

MIRLANA: I'll get it. [*She exits and Diane is finally pulled off of her son. She glares at him, panting from the exertion of trying to beat a child who is now twice her size. Dana remains seated on the couch, her face stony, blank. Deirdre goes to comfort her but Dana remains unmoved. Within seconds, Mirlana returns with Monty; he is dressed in a stylish suit, but wears no tie. His general appearance is slick.*]

*Marcus transforms instantly, greeting his agent warmly and sitting back down so that Monty has the floor.]*

MONTY: Morning, folks! Sorry I'm late!

DEMARCUS: No problem, Monty. I'm glad you're here. Mira, get the man something to drink. [*Surprised and unsure about assuming hostess duties in Diane's home, Mirlana quickly rises.*] You hungry, man? 'Cause my wife could whip you up an omelet in no time—

MONTY: No, no. I'll just take coffee—black—no sugar. [*Mirlana nods and casting an unsure glance at Diane, who makes no effort to rise, exits to kitchen. Monty claps his hands together, anxious to begin.*] So—what did I miss? [*The Gaineses look at one another but avoid Monty. Marcus laughs and the previous conflict seems to roll off him like water.*]

DEMARCUS: Just the usual family drama. But now that you're here, let's get down to business.

MONTY: [*Claps his hands together once more.*] Right! [*Since no one has offered him a seat, he drags an ottoman up to the sofa Marcus is on and sits down, his briefcase by his side.*] I've scheduled the press conference for noon on Monday.

ALVIN: Press conference?

MONTY: I think it's about time Marcus spoke to his public.

DIANE: His public?

MONTY: His fans, the league, anyone and everyone who's been following this—unfortunate incident. [*He turns back to Marcus, the only person in the room that really matters to him.*] It's important that you convey the depth of your regret over this man's misfortune—

DEMARCUS: What's the guy's name again?

MONTY: Doesn't matter, because you don't know him. Oh—and it couldn't hurt to mention the man upstairs. Nothing too preachy, just say that the victim and his family are in your prayers, and you are relying upon your own faith in God to get you through this difficult time. Finally, you need to express your willingness to assist the police in their investigation. Got it?

DEMARCUS: Got it. Uh—could you maybe write something down for me—?

MONTY: It's already done. [*Opens his briefcase and extracts a typed statement, which he hands to Marcus.*] In no way do you admit any level of participation in the altercation. You were at the club, but you were not a witness. You're nothing more than an innocent bystander, targeted by the media because of your celebrity status. [*Dana makes a sound of disgust. Monty glances at her, then continues with his agenda.*] Ok—next: I think, for the time being, we should consider dropping our suit against the league.

ALVIN: You're suing the league? What for?

MONTY: Damages. [*Mirlana enters and offers Monty a steaming cup of coffee on a saucer. Monty grins and winks at her, and takes a sip before setting the coffee precariously on the ottoman.*] Thanks, doll. That three-game suspension not only cost Marcus several hundred thousand dollars, it cost his team the series. Had Marcus been allowed to play, the team likely would have won the series, advanced to the semi-finals, and possibly won the championship.

ALVIN: I still don't see how the league is liable—

MONTY: [*Dismissive, patronizing.*] I realize all this must be rather confusing, Al—so much has changed since you were on the court. I'll try to make it simple. If Marcus had been allowed to play, if his team had been given a shot at the championship, Marcus would have been eligible for more endorsements, better trade prospects, and his jersey would have flown off the shelves. By preventing him from playing, the league effectively stripped him of his rightful earning potential by tarnishing his professional image.

DANA: Marcus tarnished his own image. He was suspended because he broke the rules.

MONTY: [*Assesses Dana and deems her a worthy adversary.*] Technically, yes. But the rules aren't always equitably enforced.

DANA: You can't possibly think this is about race—

MONTY: Not race, per se, but the league has definitely taken a more forceful position when it comes to disciplining a player whose image has been deemed…unsavory—not in keeping with the commissioner's bourgeois ideals.

ALVIN: The league has a reputation of its own to protect.

DIANE: I think it's about time they started weeding out the riff-raff. Players ought to <u>want</u> to look decent, instead of being forced to wear a suit and tie.

MONTY: [*With condescension.*] Al, Di—this isn't about decency or protecting the league.

DEIRDRE: Then what is it about?

MONTY: Race, class, and culture. [*Deirdre looks at him quizzically.*]

ALVIN: [*Disgusted.*] Thug culture.

DEMARCUS: Hip hop culture.

DANA: Oh, please…

MONTY: [*Keen to engage Dana once more.*] Profiling isn't just a tool used by racist cops. A black man working on Wall Street has to look a certain way, dress a certain way, act a certain way. If he doesn't fit the corporate profile, he's out of a job.

DANA: When you choose to join a club—or a league—or a corporation, you agree to follow their rules. You can't walk into a board room wearing a do-rag and a gold rope around your neck and expect to be taken seriously.

MARCUS: There's a rope around your neck, alright, but it's definitely not made of gold…you said it yourself, Pops—I got a mob after me.

DANA: You are not the victim here, Marcus! There's a man out there who won't ever walk again. He's paralyzed because you or one of your "associates" shot the place up!

MONTY: Actually, the shooter hasn't been identified.

DANA: Yet. [*She and Monty lock gazes. Finally, Monty looks away and puts a smarmy smile on his face.*]

MONTY: I'm sure I don't need to tell any of you how important it is that Marcus distance himself from this…tragedy. Your son—your brother—has faced a series of challenges on and off the court, and we certainly don't want to attract any more negative publicity. As his family, you have an extremely important role to play in the rehabilitation of Marcus's reputation.

DEIRDRE: What do you want us to do?

MONTY: It's a small thing, really. If contacted by the press, simply say that you have no comment, or direct them to me. [*He reaches inside his jacket and withdraws business cards, which he distributes to the Gaineses. He pretends to be addressing them all, but looks pointedly at Dana.*] It would, of course, be extremely damaging if members of Marcus's own family were to suggest that he may be guilty of attempted murder. Which, we all know, isn't true.

DANA: Speak for yourself. He cheats on his taxes, he cheats on his wife. He's cheated justice at least once before.

[*Monty scrutinizes Dana, then looks at Marcus who shrugs as if to say, "I told you so."*]

MONTY: I've retained the best criminal defense attorney in L.A.

DANA: Why? If you're so sure he's innocent.

MONTY: Guilt or innocence matters very little when your brother fits the profile: a wealthy, successful, good looking black athlete who's had previous run-ins with the criminal justice system. Marcus might as well have a bulls-eye painted on his back—he's a moving target.

DANA: Maybe he should stop moving.

MONTY: Which brings us to my next point. Our strategy to launch your career beyond the basketball court.

DEMARCUS: [*To his family.*] Monty's lined up some auditions for me. I'm thinking of going into film.

DIANE: What on earth for? I thought you were trying to avoid the spotlight.

MONTY: Different arena, Di—different spotlight. Hollywood studios are looking for someone with Marcus's qualities.

DANA: He fits the profile?

MONTY: In a matter of speaking, yes. Focus groups show that the country's ready for a black action hero. Someone who's tough, street smart, aggressive yet passionate...with that face, that physique, and that million-dollar smile, Marcus was made for the big screen.

ALVIN: What about basketball?

DEMARCUS: It's the off-season, Dad. I got plenty of time to consider my options.

ALVIN: Well, I suppose it can't hurt to try something new—so long as you remember where you belong.

DEMARCUS: And where's that, Dad?

ALVIN: On the court, Marcus! What about your motto? "All for one, and one for all"—you're ready to just abandon your team?

DEMARCUS: I told you I've been thinking about making a move.

ALVIN: A trade, you said—to another team, not another profession.

MONTY: There comes a time in every player's career when he has to stop and assess the trajectory—the path, if you will—of his own rising star. Marcus started earlier than most players—he entered the league straight out of high school and in the past ten years, he's achieved more than men twice his age: all-star, MVP, three championship rings. If it weren't for that knee injury back in 2000 and the backlash following his trial, he'd have made the U.S. Olympic team. We have to ask ourselves, what's left? What does basketball have to offer DeMarcus Gaines?

DEIRDRE: Isn't it supposed to be the other way around? "Ask not what your country can do for you…"

DEMARCUS: I've given my life to the game—to the league. I'm ready to explore other avenues. [*He glances at Monty who subtly nods with approval. The Gaineses say nothing, angering Marcus.*] It's not like I'm some dumb athlete! I can do more than dunk, you know.

DIANE: Of course you can, Marcus. You've always been bright. If you want a change, why not go back to school? I always hoped you'd go to college someday…

DEMARCUS: Ma, please. I'm too old for all that.

DEIRDRE: No, you're not, Marcus. I went back and got my degree after Tayshaun was born—remember?

DEMARCUS: That's different.

DEIRDRE: How?

DEMARCUS: Because that's you, Dee. You needed a degree in order to start your little hair styling business. I <u>am</u> my own business, see?

MONTY: DeMarcus Gaines is a brand with unparalleled and unlimited potential.

[*Diane and Alvin exchange confused, worried glances.*]

DANA: You mean he's a commodity. Something you can package and sell to the highest bidder.

MONTY: [*Shrugs helplessly.*] It is an industry...

ALVIN: My great-granddaddy had a brand. It was burned into his flesh by the man who owned him. My son is not for sale.

DEMARCUS: Dad—

ALVIN: I didn't raise him to be anybody's commodity—or anybody's slave.

MONTY: Whoa, whoa—let's not get carried away! Your analogy's all wrong, Al. In a couple of years, Marcus will be a free agent—a FREE agent. In fact, I suspect the franchise would be willing to buy out his contract right now just to avoid any more controversy.

ALVIN: And you'll see to it that Marcus is sold to the highest bidder.

MONTY: I'll see to it that your son is generously compensated for his hard work. This isn't even remotely like slavery, Al. Marcus has already earned more money than you, your father, or your father's father ever dreamt of! He's the master of his own destiny.

DEMARCUS: [*Almost surprised by the realization.*] Yeah, that's right.

MONTY: [*Goes into his briefcase and withdraws a script, which he hands to Marcus.*] Now—here's the script I was telling you about. Read it over, think about it—talk to your family, if that helps—and then let me know what you want to do. If you like it, I can arrange a screen test and a meeting with the director in the next couple of weeks.

DEMARCUS: [*Reads just the title page and frowns.*] "The Pimp King"?

MONTY: It's an urban adaptation of King Lear.

[*Dana laughs, Deirdre looks concerned.*]

DEIRDRE: You don't want Marcus to play a pimp?

MONTY: Not just any pimp—the pimp king! [*To reassure Marcus.*] It's a really meaty role—something you can sink your teeth into. Leroy—your character—has real depth, complexity. He's an outlaw, a renegade—a revolutionary!

DIANE: A pimp.

DEMARCUS: I don't know, Monty—I thought we were going for something more, like, positive.

MONTY: This film is about black power, Marcus! It's the new blaxploitation! Remember Shaft? Superfly? They were "homeboy heroes," using whatever means they had to fight the Man! The pimp today is a role model for all the young black men who can't find legitimate jobs and have to hustle just to get by. Leroy's a gangster with a heart of gold who works the system to his own advantage.

DEMARCUS: You really think this is right for me?

MONTY: I know it is.

ALVIN: Don't do it, son.

DEIRDRE: There must be other roles…

MONTY: Of course, there are other supporting roles. You could always play the dumb black sidekick to some white action hero. But this film is a vehicle for your unique talents, Marcus. You'd be the star! The script was practically written for you.

DANA: What do you mean?

MONTY: Just that the director expressly asked for an actor whose own life experiences mirror the lifestyle of the main character.

DIANE: My son is not a pimp!

MONTY: No, but he is a "baller"—in every sense of the word. We might as well capitalize off your "bad boy" reputation—you earned it. [*Even Marcus is taken aback by this shrewd remark. Monty stands and puts the ottoman back in its place. He closes his briefcase and stands.*] Well, I guess I'll head over to the hotel. I'm flying back to L.A. tonight. How about you?

DEMARCUS: [*Glances at his family and shrugs.*] Depends.

MONTY: Be on time, Marcus. The press conference starts at noon. [*Marcus smiles sheepishly. Monty turns to his "hosts" who have made no effort to rise to see him out.*] Well. Should I expect to see you folks on Monday? [*The Gaineses look at one another, but do not reply.*] That's what I thought. You know, when Marcus asked me to come out here and speak with all of you, I have to admit—I was surprised.

ALVIN: Why?

MONTY: Well, I've been representing Marcus for a number of years, and I can't say that you folks have been much of a factor in his professional life. Or his personal life, for that matter.

DEMARCUS: Monty—

DIANE: [*Outraged.*] We may not approve of all the choices he's made, but we've always been here for our son!

MONTY: Forgive me, Di, but I don't recall seeing you at the courthouse during the sexual assault trial…or at Marcus's wedding…his daughter's first birthday party… Need I go on?

DIANE: No, you need not! You've got a lot of nerve, coming into our home and talking to us like this. We're his family, and what are you? Marcus's employee!

MONTY: Technically, yes—I do work for your son, which is how you know I'm looking out for him. Marcus hired me to protect his interests and advance his career—on and off the court.

ALVIN: You want to turn Marcus into a pimp! That boy's held a ball in his hands ever since he took his first steps. Basketball's his life!

MONTY: No, Al—it's your life—or was. You can't keep living vicariously through your son. Your career ended decades ago. Marcus doesn't exist to fulfill your dreams. Not anymore.

DEMARCUS: Monty—

MONTY: If it's the money you're worried about—trust me—he can earn just as much making films.

ALVIN: I don't give a damn about the money!

MONTY: No? Then why have you suddenly decided to reconcile after turning your back on your only son for three years—three years!

DIANE: Do you have children, Mr.— [*She glances down at the business card.*] Wexler?

MONTY: As a matter of fact, I do. Two boys—eight and ten.

DIANE: Then you must know what it's like to dream for them—to want only the best things to come their way. And you must know how hard it is to sit by and watch them do something you know is a mistake.

MONTY: What I know is I would never—and I mean never—pull the kind of disappearing act you folks pulled on Marcus.

DEIRDRE: Now wait just a minute—

ALVIN: Boy, you going to stand there and let him talk to your mother that way?

DEMARCUS: Monty, chill—

MONTY: I'm sorry, Marcus. I've held my tongue these past few years, but now that I'm here, now that I see how these people treat you—

DEMARCUS: I can handle it, Monty.

ALVIN: "These people"?! Get the hell out of my house before I throw you out!

MONTY: Your house? You mean this house Marcus bought for you? You're all on some kind of allowance—

DANA: Not me!

MONTY: And what does he get in return? Marcus gives you cash, expensive gifts, access to important people. In fact, Marcus tells me you're looking for a coaching position, Al. Did you know that your son asked ME to help him find YOU a job? Did you know that, Al? Of course, you did! And you expect me to believe that this cozy little reunion is just a coincidence? Face it—you need Marcus a hell of a lot more than he needs you.

DEMARCUS: [*Finally stands and confronts Monty.*] Man—that's my father you're talking to.

MONTY: I'm your agent, Marcus. I've stood by you through the good times and the bad, but I'm not about to let you follow advice that could derail your career. Can't you see? They don't care about you!

DEMARCUS: You are my agent, Monty, and I know you got a job to do. But that man there—that's my father. And you need to show him the same respect you show me.

MONTY: No offense, Marcus, but your father's not my client.

DEMARCUS: Well, I won't be either unless I hear you apologize. Now.

MONTY: [*Monty stares at Marcus in disbelief, then glances around the room and realizes he must cede to his client's wishes. With cloying formality.*] I'm sorry, Mr. Gaines—and Mrs. Gaines—if I've offended you in any way. I only came out here because I'm concerned about your son.

ALVIN: We're concerned about our son. You're concerned about his market value.

MONTY: [*Shrugs.*] That's my job. [*There is an awkward pause, which is finally broken when Monty's cell phone goes off. Grateful for the distraction.*] Eddie! I've been trying to reach you for days. What? I told you I'd handle it. Never mind what Sorenson says—he's an idiot. I'm on it—I'm telling you, I'm on it! Listen, I'll call you right back. [*Monty ends the calls and turns to the Gaineses.*] Well, I guess I'll be going now. [*He looks to Marcus, but finds no resistance. Marcus nods and steps back to clear a path to the door. Monty nods vaguely at everyone and exits. Once he's gone, there is an awkward silence in the living room. Then Deirdre jumps up and rushes over to Marcus, clutching him in a proud embrace. Mirlana takes his hand and smiles shyly, also proud.*]

DIANE: [*Sniffs but tries to conceal her proud tears.*] Goodness--it's past noon! I'd better fix us some lunch.

MIRLANA: I'll help. [*Diane slips her arm around Mirlana's tiny waist, and Deirdre follows them toward the kitchen.*]

DEMARCUS: Got anything for the grill, Ma? I got a taste for the old man's famous whiskey barbecue sauce.

ALVIN: You ain't fooling me, boy. You're just trying to find out my secret extra-special ingredient.

DEMARCUS: [*Puts his arm around his father as they slowly move offstage.*] Aw, come on, Pops. You been promising to share that recipe with me since I was five years old.

ALVIN: I said I'd tell you when you're ready to handle that kind of classified information.

DEMARCUS: I'm ready now!

ALVIN: [*Looks at his son and for an instant, is overcome.*] Maybe you're right, son, maybe you are. [*They laugh, slap each other on the back and exit, arms wrapped around each other's shoulders. Dana watches them exit, then rises from her seat and goes over to the mantle. She examines a family portrait and sighs. As she turns to* leave the room, she spots the script lying on the sofa. Dana picks it up, scowls, but begins to read. After one page, she sinks onto the sofa, absorbed.]

## ACT II

### Scene 2

[*Dana's bedroom, later that same day. The room lacks any signs of her personality, but it is a comfortable space for a (female) guest. There is a bed with nightstand, an armoire, a dresser with mirror, and a chair with reading lamp in the corner. Dana stands by the bed, packing her suitcase in preparation for her departure. After a moment, Diane appears in the doorway. She hesitates, watches her daughter for a moment, then knocks on the open door.*]

DIANE: Can I come in?

DANA: [*Glances over her shoulder at her mother and resumes packing.*] Sure.

DIANE: [*Enters the room, trying to hide her anxiety. She straightens items on the dresser, hands Dana items from the armoire. Finally Diane comes around and sits on the bed so that she is facing Dana, although her daughter continues to ignore her.*] You don't have to leave tonight, you know.

DANA: I know.

DIANE: I was hoping we'd have more time to—

DANA: [*Stops packing for a moment.*] To what, Mom?

DIANE: [*Flushes and shifts on the bed.*] Just…to talk.

DANA: [*Resumes packing.*] We've done enough talking today to last a lifetime.

DIANE: But we didn't talk about you, Dana.

DANA: Marcus had plenty to say about me.

DIANE: [*Pause.*] Dana, I'm sorry I—I'm sorry I let him say those horrible things about you.

DANA: Don't worry about it, Mom. "Sticks and stones," right? [*Diane hangs her head, ashamed. Dana glances at her and stops packing.*] Besides, it was worth it to see you slap the spit outta his mouth.

DIANE: [*Looks at her hands as though she's never seen them before.*] I've never struck one of my children before. Your grandmother, you know, she was a church woman. "Spare the rod, spoil the child." That's how she raised us. She whipped us girls just as hard as the boys. [*She chuckles softly.*] I vowed I'd never treat my children that way. [*Pause.*] But—you were right, Dana. I did spoil your brother. I may even have ruined him.

DANA: You spared the rod, you spoiled the child—but Marcus is his own man, Mom. Remember what Monty said? "He's the master of his own destiny!"

DIANE: I just can't understand how your brother could choose to listen to that man instead of us…

DANA: [*Shrugs, weary of talking about Marcus. Continues packing.*] Monty tells Marcus what he wants to hear.

DIANE: [*Tentatively.*] I'd like to hear about your…friend.

DANA: Which one? I've got plenty of friends, Mom.

DIANE: Your lover, then.

DANA: [*Gives her mother her full attention.*] Lynn is my partner, Mom. She is my friend and my lover, but you can just say "partner."

DIANE: Alright. Things have changed so much since I was your age. I guess I have a lot to learn.

DANA: So what do you want to know?

DIANE: [*Encouraged, becomes less tentative.*] Deirdre tells me I'm going to be a grandmother again! [*She reaches out to touch Dana's hand.*] I'm so happy for you, Dana. I've always wanted you to experience motherhood.

DANA: Just not like this. [*She shakes off Diane's hand and fusses with her belongings.*]

DIANE: It's not what I imagined, but—so long as you're happy… [*Dana clenches her jaw and says nothing.*] Some of my sorors were queer! Oh—you probably don't use that word anymore.

DANA: Actually, we do. "We're queer, we're here, get used to us."

DIANE: Oh. Well, it never made any difference to me whether they had a crush on a boy or a crush on a girl. To be honest, I never really knew women had a choice until I joined the sorority. That's not the sort of thing your grandmother would have talked about.

DANA: [*Intrigued.*] There were openly gay women in your sorority?

DIANE: Well, I don't know how open they could be. But everyone knew.

DANA: How?

DIANE: They never married, or they got married and later on divorced.

DANA: Sounds like half the straight women I know.

DIANE: [*Muses to herself.*] You're right. There really isn't any difference, is there?

DANA: There is, according to the law.

DIANE: I think it's awful how they treat the queer people today—trying to change the Constitution. Fifty years ago they said a black person and a white person couldn't get married! Because <u>we</u> were subhuman, <u>we</u> weren't true citizens. We've come a long way since then, thank God.

DANA: Some of us still have a long way to go, Mom. Your "we" almost never includes me.

DIANE: [*Surprised.*] You're still black, Dana.

DANA: Of course, I am. But I'm not black the same way Dee's black. I'm not seen as a woman in the same way, and I won't be seen as a mother in the same way. I'll always be different.

DIANE: Well, you'll always be the same to me. I love you, Dana.

DANA: [*Feels Diane has missed her point and resumes packing.*] I love you, too, Mom.

DIANE: But it's not enough, is it?

DANA: [*Shrugs off her emotion.*] Beggars can't be choosers. And that's what I am in this family—a beggar. The love Marcus gets is automatic, undying, unconditional. No matter what he does, you'll never turn on him.

DIANE: [*Stunned, hurt.*] And you think we'd do that to you?

DANA: Have you seen the den lately? It's a virtual shrine to Marcus. The walls are plastered with his photographs, his awards. And where are my trophies, huh? Where are my medals, my gold? Tucked away in a corner, that's where. You don't even try to pretend that I'm worth as much as him.

DIANE: Dana! Your father and I are very proud of you—and we've always felt that way. It's just that Marcus is—well, he's different.

DANA: Special.

DIANE: All three of you are special.

DANA: Fine—he's not special, he's male.

DEMARCUS: [*From downstairs/offstage.*] Ma!

DIANE: [*Ignores him.*] I can't explain why he's so--unique...

DEMARCUS: [*Louder.*] Ma!

DIANE: All I can say is, you'll understand once you have a son of your own. The baby's due in November?

DEMARCUS: [*Louder.*] MA!

DIANE: [*Annoyed, she twists around on the bed but doesn't get up.*] Oh, for heaven's sake! I'm right here, Marcus. Quit hollering like a savage! [*Marcus enters the room, but pulls back when he sees Dana. He immediately becomes sullen.*]

DEMARCUS. Oh. That's where you are.

DIANE: Well, what is it?

DEMARCUS: [*Like a child.*] I can't find my script.

DIANE: [*Under her breath.*] Good! [*Dana goes over to the nightstand, picks up the script, and passes it to Marcus. She then resumes packing.*]

DEMARCUS: [*Eyes Dana with suspicion, and flips through the script to ensure it's intact.*] I'm surprised you didn't burn it.

DANA: [*Without turning to face him.*] It wasn't worth the match. [*Diane tries to hide a smirk but Marcus spots it and becomes petulant.*]

DEMARCUS: So that's what you two are doing up here—laughing at me behind my back, huh?

DIANE: Boy, your head's so big, it may not even fit on the silver screen. We were NOT talking about you.

DEMARCUS: Yeah, well…it's MY script. I should've got to read it before anyone else.

DIANE: Oh, hush! Your hands were covered in barbecue sauce, anyway. Between the two of you, you ate the whole damn cow. Where's your father?

DEMARCUS: 'Sleep.

DIANE: [*She turns to Dana.*] So, Dana, what did you think of "The Pimp King"? Thumbs up or thumbs down? [*Dana, sensing her mother's mischievous mood, dares to look over at Marcus.*]

DANA: There might be a role in there for Mirlana. [*Marcus bristles.*] But you won't like it, Mom—lots of cursing, and "we be goin' to the sto'," and "dis 'n dat 'n dem 'n dose." [*To Marcus.*] You'll need to take a crash course in Ebonics before your screen test.

DIANE: Not quite what the Bard had in mind, I'm sure.

DEMARCUS: [*Drawn in despite himself.*] So, how's it end?

DANA: He dies.

DIANE: How?

DANA: [*Zips up her suitcase and sets it on the floor next to the bed.*] Leroy throws himself in front of a bus to save his one loyal 'ho.

DIANE: [*Diane coughs lightly to cover her laughter.*] Death by bus. How noble.

DEMARCUS: [*Sucks his teeth.*] Whatever. I'm outta here. [*He turns to go but Diane calls him back.*]

DIANE: Marcus?

DEMARCUS: Yeah?

DIANE: Your sister's leaving soon. [*Marcus simply nods at the suitcase and turns to go. Diane calls him back again.*] Son?

DEMARCUS: What, Ma? [*She looks at him sternly and he rearranges his scowl.*]

DIANE: Aren't you going to say goodbye?

DEMARCUS: [*Looks at his mother, then glances at Dana, whose back is turned to him.*] Bye.

DIANE: [*Quickly, to keep Marcus engaged.*] The next time you see Dana, she'll probably be holding your brand new nephew. The baby's due around Thanksgiving. You and Mirlana will be here for Thanksgiving, won't you?

DEMARCUS: I don't know, Ma.

DIANE: [*Disappointed.*] Oh. [*Refocuses on Dana.*] You'd better congratulate your sister now, then. [*Marcus rolls his eyes and Diane forcefully turns Dana to face him. They still avoid eye contact.*] Go on.

DEMARCUS: [*Doesn't want to disrespect his mother, but also doesn't want to yield. There is an awkward pause.*] What do you want me to say, Ma? "Way to go, Dana!" It's like some twisted lesbo version of Home Ec. They pay some guy to squirt in a cup, add a couple of eggs, and hope the baby looks okay when it comes out the oven.

DANA: I guess I should have looked for a "real man" like you, a big, black stud who sows his wild oats all over the damn place.

DEMARCUS: At least I make my babies the old fashioned way.

DIANE: [*Gets between them like a referee.*] That's enough, you two! I'm so sick of this ridiculous rivalry. Sit down!

DEMARCUS: What?

DIANE: I said, sit down—both of you! [*Reluctantly, Dana sinks onto the bed and Marcus takes a seat in a corner armchair.*] Now, I'm going to leave the room. I'm going to stand on the other side of that door, and you're not coming out until you've managed to have a civil conversation.

DANA: Mom, my flight leaves a couple of hours.

DIANE: Then you'd better get busy.

DEMARCUS: Ma— [*Diane exits, slamming the door behind her. Taking a chair from down the hall, Diane stations herself outside the* bedroom, arms folded.  Inside, Dana checks her watch and fumes; Marcus makes a similar sound of disgust.  For a full minute, they say nothing to one another. Finally Marcus approaches the door, and listens.*]

DIANE:  I'm waiting!

[*Marcus flings himself back into the chair.  Dana checks her watch again and sighs resignedly.*]

DANA:  Alright, look.  The only way we're getting out of here is if she hears us talking.  So talk.

DEMARCUS:  I ain't got nothing to say.

DANA:  For once!  Well, I have a plane to catch. [*She gets up, snatches the script from his hand, and opens it up.*]

DEMARCUS:  Hey!

DANA:  Get up.

DEMARCUS:  No!

DANA:  You want to get out of this room?  Then get up, and read the damn script.  Maybe she'll think we're "getting along." [*Marcus hesitates, then hauls himself up and steps closer to Dana.  She holds the script at arm's length so he can see.*] I'll play… Reba.  You play Leroy.

DEMARCUS: [*Snickers.*]  Why don't you play Gonerilla. [*Dana glares at him and Marcus settles down.*] "Yo, bitch!  Where's my money?"

DANA:  "I don' work fo' you no mo', muthafucka."

DEMARCUS:  "The hell you don't." [*He stops and grins.*]  I'm supposed to slap you.

DANA: [*Death stare.*]  Keep reading.

[*Diane frowns, and puts her ear to the door.*]

DEMARCUS: [*Tries to assume the role of a pimp, but stumbles over the crass language.*] "Afta all I done fo' you, dis is how you pay me back?  I dragged yo' ass outta the gutta.  I slapped a weave on yo' nappy head—got yo' nails did—dressed yo' skanky ass up like a lady. 'N you sell me out t' dat dumb cop, Eddie?"

DANA: [*Sighs, reads in a flat tone.*] "You ain't nuthin but a punk-ass bitch, Leroy. You ain't neva done nuthin fo' me. I sell my pussy every day and you jus' take my money 'n treat me like a dog. I know you been two timin' me, Leroy. You likes Carmella better 'n me! I'm yo' bitch, Leroy—me! Not her! [*Dana shoves the script at Marcus and sinks back onto the bed. She falls back and groans.*] I give up! We're just going to have to sit here in silence until Mom lets us out.

DEMARCUS: What about the script? We were just getting started.

DANA: I can't read that crap, Marcus. It hurts my tongue—not to mention my dignity.

DEMARCUS: [*Shakes the script at her and nearly pleads.*] Come on, Dane, let's just finish this scene. You say, "I'm yo' bitch, Leroy—me! Not her!" And then I say— [*He pauses and loses his enthusiasm.*] "Suck my dick, bitch." [*Marcus sighs and then hurls the script at the wall. Dana jumps at the sound and props herself up on her elbows.*]

DANA: I know you don't want my advice, Marcus, but you can do better than that. Plus it'd break Mom's heart to see you play Leroy, "The Pimp King."

DEMARCUS: [*Sinks into the corner chair.*] Yeah, well, you can't please all the people all the time. I take this role—I get seen on screen. In Hollywood, it's all about visibility. You can't just sit at home and wait for the perfect role to fall into your lap.

DANA: It means that much to you—becoming a movie star?

DEMARCUS: What else am I going to do?

DANA: You're young, Marcus! You're nowhere near your prime. Unless your knee gives out again, you've got at least another ten years on the court.

DEMARCUS: [*Pause.*] I used to think basketball was everything. Winning meant everything.

DANA: So what changed?

DEMARCUS: I don't know. It's just not enough any more.

DANA: [*Sighs.*] The thrill is gone. [*She rolls onto her side and props her head on her folded arm. Marcus darts his eyes at her but Dana is tracing the pattern on the flowery bedspread. Somehow that makes him feel it's safe to speak.*]

DEMARCUS: Is that what happened to you?

DANA: [*Pause.*] Sort of. I wanted to end my career on a high note, not end up on a highlight reel, getting a facial from one of those seven-foot rookies from Eastern Europe.

DEMARCUS: [*Laughs.*] Yeah. [*Grows serious again.*] You don't miss being out on the court?

DANA: I do when my team is losing! I'll always love basketball. But coaching shows me just how much I still have to learn about the game. You could coach.

DEMARCUS: [*Shakes his head.*] Nah.

DANA: Well, if you really want to be on camera, you could always get a job as a sportscaster. The networks would pay big bucks for a star like you.

DEMARCUS: Yeah, I've thought about it. But I don't want to get stuck with a bunch of old-timers talking about the good old days of afros and short-shorts. [*Dana laughs despite herself.*] Sometimes…

DANA: [*Dana prompts him gently.*] Yeah?

DEMARCUS: Sometimes I wish Mom and Pops had made me go to college. Sometimes I feel like I've missed half my life.

DANA: It was a hard decision for them. You were young, but you were so talented. You were a prodigy, Marcus.

DEMARCUS: If I was your son, what would you have done?

DANA: God, I don't know. Part of me would want to protect you…and part of me would want you to shine. [*Pause.*] You're one of the greatest players of all time, Marcus. You know that, right?

DEMARCUS: [*Looks down at his hands.*] It gets lonely sometimes.

DANA: Yeah, I guess it would. You're in a league of your own.

DEMARCUS: [*Bitterly.*] A league of one. [*They sit in sympathetic silence for a moment.*] You know, I always used to look up to you. When we were kids.

DANA: Yeah, right. By the time you were ten, you were already taller than me!

DEMARCUS: That's not what I mean. [*Shyly.*] You were, like, my role model. [*Dana looks at him skeptically, and Marcus strives to convince her he is sincere.*] I mean, Dad—he was my coach. He taught me the basic skills, made me stay focused, taught me to be disciplined. But you—you were the best player I knew. Nobody could handle the ball like my big sister.

DANA: [*Still mildly resentful.*] You dunked on me when you were twelve.

DEMARCUS: [*Laughs.*] I remember that day. I thought I'd finally arrived. I was finally as good as you. And then you wiped the court with my ass.

DANA: I had to teach you a lesson. You were getting uppity.

DEMARCUS: You sure schooled me that day. [*Pause. He squirms uncomfortably in the small chair.*] You made me the player I am today, Dane.

DANA: [*Shakes her head dismissively.*] You've earned every bit of your success, Marcus. You were always driven, even as a kid.

DEMARCUS: Because I wanted you to respect me.

DANA: You definitely became a worthy opponent.

DEMARCUS: I didn't want to be your opponent, Dana. [*Quietly.*] I wanted to be on your team. [*Diane, who has been seated outside the door listening, creeps away satisfied. Dana blushes, and cannot bring herself to look at her brother.*] When did I become your enemy?

DANA: [*Ashamed.*] I don't know.

DEMARCUS: Was there ever a time when you liked me?

DANA: When it was just you and me, it was okay—better than okay. But whenever anyone else came around—even Dee—it was like I disappeared. I didn't matter anymore because the only one they could see was you.

DEMARCUS: Everyone knew you were the better player.

DANA: Maybe. But you were the son. [*Pause.*]

DEMARCUS: You excited about this baby?

DANA: Excited. Terrified.

DEMARCUS: I didn't think you'd want a boy.

DANA: I didn't, at first. But after three miscarriages, it didn't matter any more. All we want is a healthy baby.

DEMARCUS: Yeah. I know what that's like. Mirlana thinks she owes me a son, but it's not like that.

DANA: Your girls are beautiful. You going to teach them to play ball?

DEMARCUS: Are you kidding? They got a hoop in the bedroom, a hoop in the basement, a full court in the backyard…[*Dana smiles at him.*] My girls are going to grow up to be just like their aunty. The Great Dane.

DANA: You still think I'm a good role model?

DEMARCUS: [*Looks away.*] Sure.

DANA: I'll make you a deal, Marcus. I won't bring Lynn and the baby here for Thanksgiving if you promise to hold off on your screen test until a decent script comes along.

DEMARCUS: [*Offended.*] Why can't I meet her?

DANA: [*Surprised.*] You want to?

DEMARCUS: She's family now, right? I've seen her around. She's cute.

DANA: You sound surprised. [*Marcus shrugs guiltily, and Dana smiles despite herself. Then she glances at her watch and jumps up from the bed.*] Oh, shit! I'm going to miss my flight. [*Marcus rises and checks the door.*]

DEMARCUS: Coast is clear. [*He comes back into the room and grabs Dana's suitcase.*] I'll take this downstairs.

DANA: [*Flustered, is hurriedly scanning the room and gathering the last of her belongings.*] Thanks. Marcus— [*He stops at the doorway and turns around.*] Listen, if things don't work out—I mean, this shooting—if it doesn't go away…[*He looks at her expectantly, but Dana falters, unsure what to say.*] You're my kid brother, Marcus. The only one I've got. I know you and Dee are tight and everything, but—if you need me, I can be there. Just let me know, okay?

DEMARCUS: Okay. [*He turns, and exits carrying the suitcase. Troubled, Dana watches him go, and checks her watch once more. She paces the room for a moment, then, as she is about to leave, catches her reflection in the mirror. She sits down on the bed and takes a deep breath. After a moment, she digs inside her purse and finds her cell phone. She hits speed dial and Lynn answers almost right away.*]

DANA: Hey, hon, it's me. How you feeling? Yeah? That's good. Uh—yeah, I'm ok. Well, it hasn't exactly been a picnic, but—I think we're making progress. At least, I hope we are. Listen, babe, I think I'm going to stay a couple days longer. Are you okay with that? Are you sure? I hate leaving you alone like this, but I think—I think my brother needs me.

## ACT II

## Scene 3

[*A table is set up for a press conference. Reporters and photographers anxiously await DeMarcus's arrival. Next to the microphone positioned in the center of the table is a pitcher of water and three empty glasses to go with the three empty chairs. Monty, dressed in a suit and tie, enters first, followed by DeMarcus and Mirlana. Flash bulbs go off. Marcus is also in a suit. Mirlana wears a fitted designer suit that is more modest than her usual attire. Despite the glare of the flash, she is not wearing sunglasses. All three have a serious, business-like demeanor. As soon as they are seated at the table, Dana enters, followed by Alvin, Diane, and Deirdre. They stand behind those who are seated. There is a murmur from the crowd of reporters. Marcus takes a deep breath, and draws the microphone closer. He takes up the printed statement Monty has written for him and clears his throat.*]

DEMARCUS: [*Reads directly from the paper.*] "Good afternoon. I'd like to start by thanking all of you for coming here today. The past few weeks have been extremely difficult for me and my family. Many untrue and unfair statements have been made about me, and I appreciate this opportunity to set the record straight." [*Pause. Monty nods at Marcus encouragingly. Marcus hesitates, then clears his throat once more and goes on.*] "I would like to offer my sympathy to the victim of last week's shooting at the Prince's Palace. My thoughts and prayers go out to him and his family, and I sincerely hope that God will give them the strength they need to deal with this tragedy.

As for me—" [*Pause. Again, Monty urges him on, but Marcus is slow to respond. Concerned, Diane steps forward and places a hand on her son's shoulder. Marcus bites his lip and sets the statement down.*] I can't do this.

MONTY: [*Reaches out a hand and covers the microphone.*] Marcus? What's happening? [*Marcus shakes his head but makes no reply.*] Talk to me, Marcus.

[*Alvin steps up and puts his hand on his son's other shoulder. Dana and Deirdre hold onto their parents, forming a unified front. Marcus crumples up the statement, which rolls away from him and falls from the table. Mirlana reaches over and takes her husband's hand. Marcus, momentarily overcome, composes himself, and then pushes Monty's hand away from the microphone.*]

DEMARCUS: Alright, everybody, listen up. I got something I need to say.

## THE END

# A TALK WITH THE PLAYWRIGHT

An interview conducted by Carolyn nur Wistrand

**ZETTA ELLIOTT** earned her PhD in American Studies from NYU. Her poetry has been published in the Cave Canem anthology, *The Ringing Ear: Black Poets Lean South*, *Check the Rhyme: an Anthology of Female Poets and Emcees*, and *Coloring Book: an Eclectic Anthology of Fiction and Poetry by Multicultural Writers*. Her novella, *Plastique*, was excerpted in *T Dot Griots: an Anthology of Toronto's Black Storytellers*, and her essays have appeared in *The Black Arts Quarterly*, *thirdspace*, *WarpLand* and *Rain and Thunder*. She won the 2005 Honor Award in Lee & Low Books' New Voices Contest, and her picture book, *Bird*, was published in October 2008. Her first play, *Nothing but a Woman*, was a finalist in the Chicago Dramatists' Many Voices Project (2006). Her fourth full-length play, *Connor's Boy*, was staged in January 2008 as part of two new play festivals: in Cleveland, OH as part of Karamu House's R. Joyce Whitley Festival of New Plays ARENAFEST, and in New York City as part of Maieutic Theatre Works' Newborn Festival. Her one-act play, *girl/power*, was staged as part of New Perspectives Theater's festival of women's work, GIRLPOWER, in August 2008. She is currently a visiting professor in the African American and African Studies Program at Mt. Holyoke College.

**Q: How did you begin writing?**

According to the old report cards my mother saved, I've been telling stories since I was a little girl. I remember consciously starting to write for English class in high school (Grade Ten). My teacher, Ms. Nancy Vichert, read my stories, which I paired with dramatic pictures cut from magazines, and she said, "If you want to be a writer, you will be." She made it seem so simple, like all I had to do was make the decision and it would happen. So when I was 15 I started writing my first novel. That went nowhere, but I kept writing non-fiction; I took lots of literature courses in college, and my professors were very generous with their praise. Once I discovered Toni Morrison and

Jamaica Kincaid, I realized black women writers really did exist, and then I started writing for real. I graduated from college in '93, went to visit my father in Brooklyn, NY that summer, and returned to Toronto that fall with an outline for my first novel. I didn't finish it until 1999, but I did it and there was no stopping me after that.

**Q: When did you know you were going to be a writer?**

It actually took a long time for me to claim that identity. I *felt* like I was a writer, but it was a secret passion—not something I felt comfortable claiming in public. In part b/c so often when you say, "I'm a writer," people's first question is: "What have you published?" So for a long time I thought I couldn't call myself a writer without a published book. In graduate school, almost all of my friends were writers but they had more confidence (and success!) than I had. I'd been writing essays for so long, and I'm a mimic—so I easily reproduce the tone of whatever I've been reading. It wasn't hard to write scholarly papers when I was constantly reading books and articles by scholars. But midway through graduate school I had a crisis—I didn't actually want to be an academic, and another grad student called me out and suggested I was being disingenuous. I did feel like a fraud in some ways, so I decided to quit altogether. My Chair convinced me to take a one-year leave instead, and I finally finished that novel I'd started back in '93. I had no job, I was depending on the kindness of my family members, and every day I'd just get up and write. I sent chapters to editors and agents, and got a positive response…I thought I'd arrived! So in that moment I felt really committed to writing. But when no contract arrived, I realized I had a problem. I spent 4 months just trying to get publishers to notice me, and finally I realized I had to move on. That's when I started writing for children. A few years later I heard Toni Morrison give a talk in Minnesota and she said, "You don't need anyone's permission to be a writer." You need that permission to be an *author*, but not a writer. And so I think moving on after that first novel was a pivotal moment for me. I write b/c it's necessary for me, and the experience itself—even more than the finished project—is enough. It's preparation for what's next. And that may or may not be a published book or a produced play.

**Q: How do you balance your work in the academy with your creative writing?**

It's very difficult. I think I accepted after a time that I didn't want to be an academic. And once I accepted that truth, I stopped trying to prove myself in the expected ways. I stopped writing scholarly essays and focused on my fiction; when I did write essays, I wrote something hybrid—something that reflected my identity as an artist in the academy. The academy isn't so different from the corporate world—you can run up on some cut throat, competitive people, and you can feel like you're being tested *all* the time. As a woman of color who looks much younger than I actually am, I find I'm often patronized and dismissed by older scholars. I respond to this by enforcing a split between my JOB and my LIFE. I teach b/c I'm passionate about learning, and to teach is to learn. It's also a way to support my writing; I have a flexible schedule, and enough time to complete my writing projects. But I can't spend too much time in the academy—it's great to be around other people who value reading, and writing, and the exchange of ideas. But there's still bias—a feeling that artists aren't intellectuals, or that the work (most living) artists produce isn't rigorous or legitimate. So I'm careful about the folks I spend time with. I have wonderful friends in the academy, but my closest friends are artists—they put no limits on me.

**Q: Is there anyone in particular that you look on as a key influence?**

I think my artist-friends have been a major influence on me…they provide me with community, they inspire me, they encourage me, they accept me. When I started writing for children, I met an editor, Laura Atkins, who invited me out to lunch and told me I had a really distinctive voice; I never published a book with her, but we're still friends, and she's still coaching me! When I started sending out poetry, Nikky Finney read my work and sent me the kindest messages—I expected her to seriously edit my work, but instead she said it needed to stay just the way it was; she encouraged me to claim my identity as a poet, and I still haven't, but she made me feel welcome. When I started writing plays, David Alan Moore became an important person—he was so genuine and kind, and he praised my first play so sincerely...then he read an essay I had published online, and wrote to tell me he identified with my struggle to find a place in the professional world. He's so accomplished but so humble; he wrote letters of recommendation for me, and made me feel like I had the right to call myself a playwright. When you write across different genres, you run the risk of not being taken seriously in *any* field, so it's important to get that validation from folks "in the know." When I first met Carolyn nur Wistrand, she immediately opened up to me—that kind of reception is so important—to *not* be shut down, or shut out. She didn't see me as an upstart or a novice, she immediately offered praise and advice and became an invaluable mentor. Established artists sometimes see emerging artists as competition, but I've been blessed to have mentors who truly want me to succeed.

**Q: What is the process by which something you write becomes something that works onstage?**

I don't know if I'm qualified to answer that. As a playwright, I don't have a whole lot of say when it comes to how my work is staged, and I'm often more concerned with how the piece works on the page. I'm just trying to tell a story that's authentic and compelling. I'm working on my eighth full-length play right now, and I think it wasn't until my fourth play (*Connor's Boy*) that I started to understand dramatic writing. I have very little experience in the theatre world—I don't attend many plays, and I only started reading plays in the last couple of years in order to learn more about the form. I find dialogue compelling; I come from a family where people don't generally speak openly about how they feel, and so I use writing as a way of rectifying that situation. Even folks in the street will say, "Don't even GO there!" and I think, "Why not?" Maybe we *need* to go there...in order to move forward, in order to really connect with one another, or to be our true selves. I think honesty works—it's almost inherently dramatic, b/c people fear the truth, and they go through so many different machinations to avoid facing and/or speaking it. And the truth hurts, quite often. I think successful plays have characters with whom we identify in some way—we may not like the character, but we see a part of ourselves in their vulnerability, or their hostility, or their pain. I tend to write about dysfunctional families, so ALL of those aspects are present...

**Q: *Mother Load* has appeal to a multi-generational theatre audience. Is this a family story?**

Yes, I'd consider it a family drama. I write mostly about families, but I'm particularly interested in relationships between women. So I write about sisters quite a bit, and mothers/daughters. I think I'm somewhat obsessed with the stories we're sold about women and their relationship to one another (in advertising especially). I wasn't close to my mother or my older sister, and yet I'm very close to my female friends; in some ways, I've spent my life looking for "other mothers" and other sisters. I think women betray and terrorize one another fairly often—just as often as we uplift and nurture and support one another. Add a man to the mix and it gets really tricky sometimes...*Mother Load* was a way to examine competition between women, and to tackle that myth of motherhood—that all women have this "natural instinct" to reproduce, and nurture, and sacrifice their lives for their kids. I've read some weighty books about healing the rift between mothers and daughters, and before writing this play, I read Rebecca Walker's book about becoming a mother (*Baby Love*). I was surprised that even before I opened her book, I had sided with her mother (Alice Walker). I then had to ask myself why I did that, when I tend to see my own difficult relationship with my mother as *her* fault, not mine. I'm a feminist; my mother is, in my mind, a patriarchal woman. I wondered how much of a woman's identity was the result of her decision to emulate or oppose her own mother. Elders are so important in black communities, yet their attitudes towards the young are sometimes problematic. I wanted to consider continuity and conflict between generations of women—to see if I could stand in another woman's shoes for a moment.

**Q: Your work questions and challenges the status of women in contemporary society. Is this a conscious act in how you construct characters?**

Well, I'm a feminist, so I'm always conscious of the status of women (I like to think so, anyway). I'm invested in women's perspectives, and the challenges many women face. *Connor's Boy* was, again, a meditation on motherhood...who's "qualified" to become a mother? I have an older adopted brother who was returned to his birth mother after living with my family for four years. I saw how his life was negatively impacted by the decisions my parents and his birth parents made. And I recalled my maternal grandfather once saying that my brother was "just a bad seed." I was so infuriated, yet when I think about that phrase, I see how it implicates the birth *mother* especially. Women are blamed for so much—burdened so heavily when it comes to parenting, and then faulted for being less than perfect. But I think most mothers want to be good parents. So why do so many fail? In the black community, transracial adoption has been an issue for decades—and now gay adoption is as well. I think as a community we've yet to have the really substantive, honest discussions we need to have about hybridity. We rely on essentialist assumptions—(straight) black parents are best suited to raise black children—and we give ourselves a pass on homophobia by dressing it up as some kind of radical black nationalism. If we truly love black children, what's the best way to demonstrate that love? Holding on, or letting go? Maybe a little bit of both...

**Q: Your short play, *girl/power*, was recently produced at New Perspectives Theatre in New York City in the Women's Work Festival. What was the reaction of the audience to this piece?**

From what I could see, there was a fair bit of laughter. Girl 1 was comical at times, and her personality differed so much from Girl 2 that the audience found that amusing. It's hard to gauge someone else's response without talking to him or her directly, and there wasn't a talk-back after the play was over. I prefer written reviews of my work, really, b/c then you know exactly what someone thought or felt, and usually people put more thought into what they write. There's also a difference between what I write and what people see during a performance of my play. The latter depends mostly on the actors and the director, who are interpreting the script.

**Q. You recently stated that many of your plays were, "ripped from the headlines." Could you elaborate on this statement?**

I took that from *Law & Order*, which is one of my favorite television programs. I actually watch a lot of TV these days, and I think that's partly how I've learned to write compelling dialogue. "Ripped from the headlines" means I'm trying to address something that's happening NOW. When you write with the intent to publish, you can generally expect a pretty long wait; I wrote my children's book, BIRD, in 2002, and it's just now coming out in 2008. That lag really aggravates me, b/c often the moment is lost…the writing may still be good, but it won't resonate with readers in the same way b/c the topic is no longer current or at the front of their minds. I think writing reflects our culture in a particular moment—and it's a reflection of who I am right now, too—I look back at things I wrote years ago, and I remember who I was then, what I was going through, why I tackled a particular topic. I now self-publish b/c I'm tired of waiting for traditional publishers to give me their stamp of approval. I can write a play and have it available for sale online almost immediately. The sooner the work gets out into the world, the sooner folks can start talking about it; my plays haven't yet been produced, but they still have value (for me, anyway!) and may resonate with readers instead of theatre-goers.

**Q: How does your ability to write in mixed genre influence you as a playwright?**

Well, writing in different genres means you're always a beginner and when you're starting out, you're generally less afraid to take risks. There's an idea that you have to "master" a form to be truly proficient otherwise you're a dilettante, a jack-of-all-trades (master of none). I'm not really interested in mastery—I think it's an antiquated idea (and elitist, too). I think a curious mind reaches for whatever's beyond its grasp. I don't go see many plays, and I've never studied acting; I approach playwriting from a different place, and to some, that makes me an automatic failure or an aberration, an outsider. I think I bring something different to the table—a different perspective, different reference points, different intent. And perhaps other playwrights can learn from me just as I learn from them. I tend to write quickly as well, so in three years I've written twenty plays; I think pretty soon I'll have learned what I needed to learn from this genre, and I'll apply that to whatever I start writing next—maybe screenplays (I've written one so far). Writing in different genres teaches you about yourself—your strengths, your limitations. You also become more sensitive to audiences, I think. I never assume that everything I write is for everyone. And I like to surprise people—I'm *always* underestimated, so pushing myself is a way of showing others just what I can do. I walk into a theatre for rehearsal and no one assumes that I'm the playwright. But maybe once they see me there often enough, they'll start to think differently about black women—maybe they won't assume we're all video 'hos or aspiring actresses. Better yet, maybe they'll stop making assumptions about us—period!

**Q: What lies down the road?**

I don't know because I haven't gotten there yet! I try to take things one step at a time. I have anxiety issues, so trying to predict the future isn't good for me. My children's picture book comes out in October, and so I imagine I'll be working with younger children again, and I'm looking forward to that. I intend to continue teaching at the college level, and my contract's nearly up at my current job, so I'll have to start looking for another—that will likely involve moving out of the northeast. I want to finish this last play, and maybe revisit my screenplay. I want to learn how to make short films. I'm trying to promote my memoir and young adult novel. Most importantly, I need to ensure that I'm getting my work done. I try to follow James Baldwin's advice to writers: "The point is to get your work done, and your work is to change the world."

**Q: Why do we need the voices of black female playwrights?**

Black feminists have been saying for decades that if you listen to US, all the problems of this society will be fixed, b/c we're at the bottom and we KNOW what we're talking about! A Canadian writer, Marlene Nourbese Phillip, suggested that being on the margins is actually empowering...marginalized people are potentially cutting edge, avant garde, precisely b/c we're tottering at the lip of the page—we're not secure in the center. People often see black women as powerless, or clueless, or disinterested in politics. If we are silent, others often assume we have nothing to say. And even some black men have tried to silence us, fearing we'll tell tales that implicate them. But we have important stories to tell, we have a unique perspective b/c we are unique beings, and we are uniquely positioned to tell others about themselves—and about ourselves, too! A black woman might just be the next First Lady of the United States. The media claims the American public wants to know more about Michelle Obama. She wouldn't be such a mystery to them if they spent more time reading black woman authors instead of settling for the stereotypical representations on TV. Black woman playwrights dramatize life—they open a window into a world that more people need to occupy or at least be aware of.

**CAROLYN NÚR WISTRAND**'s plays have been staged at the Nat Horne Theatre, Harold Clurman Theatre, Arthur Seelen Theatre, and Open Eye: New Stagings in New York City, The Bilingual Foundation for the Arts, Los Angeles, California, Around the Coyote, Chicago, Illinois, The Charles H. Wright Museum of African American History, Detroit, Michigan, The Georgia World Congress Center, Atlanta, Georgia, and The Phoenix Civic Plaza, Phoenix, Arizona. Published plays include: *Beauty in Black Performance: Plays for African American Youth* (Africa World Press) *Ida B. 'n The Lynching Tree: A Record of Race History & Mean Molly: An African Folktale of the Deep South*, (One Act Play Depot, Canada); *Before the Spanish Came,* (Contemporary Drama Service), and *Táhirih,* (Carmel Publishers, Chandigarh, India). In 2006 she collaborated with South African poet and activist, Dennis Brutus (imprisoned with Nelson Mandela on Robben Island) on an original staging of his poem, *Sirens, Knuckles, and Boots,* and in 2007 she adapted Egyptian feminist, Nawaal El Saadawi's novel, *Woman at Point Zero,* for the stage. She is a member of The Dramatists Guild, ICWP, and the Schomburg Center for Research in Black Culture. She is currently a faculty member in the Department of Africana Studies, University of Michigan-Flint.